ERNESTO ... GUEVARA was b.. ...na in
19... After fighting alongside Fidel C... ..he three-
year guerrilla war in Cuba, he became Minister for
Industry following the victory of the Cuban revolution.
In 1966 he established a ... ...via. He
was captured an...

Visit www.A... ...ve
information on y... ...thors.

From the reviews of *The Motorcycle Diaries*:

'*Das Kapital* meets *Easy Rider*'   The Times

'A Latin American James Dean or Jack Kerouac'
                                      Washington Post

'A journey, a number of journeys. Ernesto Guevara in
search of adventure, Ernesto Guevara in seach of
America, Ernesto Guevara in search of Che. On this
journey of journeys, solitude found solidarity. "I"
turned into "we"'   EDUARDO GALEANO

'An extraordinary first-person account. If the world
eventually came to know Che Guevara and his New
Man, in *The Motorcycle Diaries* we see the formative man.
It redoubles his image and lends a touch of humanity
with enough rough edges to invite controversy'
                          Los Angeles Times Book Review

'For every comic escapade of the carefree roustabout there is an equally eye-opening moment in the development of the future revolutionary leader. By the end of the journey, a politicized Guevara has emerged to predict his own legendary future' *Time*

'There is pathos in these pages – the pathos of Che himself, ever thoughtful, ever willing to sacrifice all, burning with guilt over his own privileges and never letting his sufferings impede him' *New Yorker*

'*The Motorcycle Diaries* mixes lyrical observation, youthful adventure and anti-imperialist political analysis . . . This candid journal, part self-discovery, part fieldwork, glimmers with portents of the future revolutionary'
Publishers Week

'Che is certainly a shrewd observer of what he calls the "strange" human race . . . The great thing about this book is that Che Guevara is never a bore. It satisfies both as an enjoyable travelogue and as a chronicle of the development of one of this century's most romantic figures' *Literary Review*

'What distinguishes these diaries . . . is that they reveal a human side to El Che which historians have successfully managed to suppress. It is in the pages of this breathless journal . . . that one senses El Che's belief that determination and conviction can be enough to change one's self and others . . . The journal . . . is a joy to read from start to finish' *Financial Times*

'A revolutionary bestseller . . . It's true, Marxists just wanna have fun'   *Guardian*

'This journey was obviously the formative influence on Che's Pan-Americanism and the development of his revolutionary consciousness . . . There's political incorrectness galore . . . this book should do much to humanize the image of a man who found his apotheosis as a late '60s cultural icon. It is also, incidentally, a remarkably good travel book about South America'   *The Scotsman*

'The vision of the noble loner, whether freedom-fighter or biker . . . gives hope to world-weary revolutionaries and non-revolutionaries alike'   *Weekend Telegraph*

'Politically correct revolutionary hero? Perhaps a few years later, but in this account Che Guevara comes over as one of the lads'   *Bike*

'This book is worth reading for more than novelty value. In his journey across Latin America, through the Andes and the rainforest, Che's diary is full of original observation, hilarious mishaps and human understanding'   *Briefing*

'Che writes with wit and skill, giving insights into the world that shaped his beliefs . . . The reader can see him piecing together the ideas that will shape his political future'   *Impact*

ERNESTO
CHE GUEVARA

the motorcycle diaries
NOTES ON A LATIN AMERICAN JOURNEY

Preface by Aleida Guevara March
Introduction by Cintio Vitier

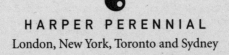

HARPER PERENNIAL
London, New York, Toronto and Sydney

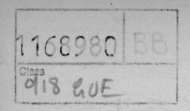
Harper Perennial
An imprint of HarperCollins*Publishers*
77–85 Fulham Palace Road
Hammersmith
London W6 8JB

www.harperperennial.co.uk

This *Stranger Than . . .* edition published by Harper Perennial 2007

1

First published in paperback in 2003 by Ocean Press, Australia
First published in Great Britain in 2004 by Fourth Estate
Published in paperback by Harper Perennial 2004 and reprinted 10 times

Copyright © 2003 Che Guevara Studies Center
Copyright © 2003 Aleida March
Published under license from Ocean Press
Preface translated by Julie Wark
Photographs copyright © Aleida March, Che Guevara Studies Center and Ocean Press

The right of Alexandra Keeble to be identified as the translator of this work has been
asserted by her in accordance with the Copyright, Designs and Patents Act 1988

A catalogue record for this book is available from the British Library

ISBN-13 978-0-00-724171-2
ISBN-10 0-00-724171-2

Printed and bound in Great Britain by Clays Ltd, St Ives plc

contents

Preface, *by Aleida Guevara March*   1

Preface to the first edition, *by Aleida March*   4

Ernesto Che Guevara   5

Brief chronology of Ernesto Che Guevara   7

Map and Itinerary of *The Motorcycle Diaries*   11

Introduction, *by Cintio Vitier*   15

the motorcycle diaries

So we understand each other   *31*

Forewarnings   *32*

The discovery of the ocean   *34*

...Lovesick pause   *35*

Breaking the last tie   *38*

For the flu: bed   *40*

San Martín de los Andes   *44*

Circular exploration   *47*

Dear Mama   *50*

The seven lakes road   *51*

And now, I feel my great roots unearth, free and...   *53*

Curious objects   *55*

"The Experts"   57

The difficulties intensify   60

La Poderosa II's final tour   62

Firefighters, workers and other matters   64

La Gioconda's smile   67

Stowaways   73

This time, disaster   76

Chuquicamata   79

Arid land for miles and miles   82

The end of Chile   84

Chile, a vision from afar   86

Tarata, the new world   89

In the dominion of Pachamama   94

Lake of the sun   98

Toward the navel of the world   100

The navel!   103

The land of the Incas   105

Lord of the earthquakes   111

Homeland for the victor   113

Cuzco straight   115

Huambo   118

Ever northward   123

Through the center of Peru   126

Shattered hopes   129

The city of the viceroys   133

Down the Ucayali   *140*

Dear Papi   *145*

The San Pablo leper colony   *146*

Saint Guevara's day   *148*

Debut for the little Kontiki   *152*

Dear Mama   *153*

On the road to Caracas   *158*

This strange twentieth century   *160*

A note in the margin   *163*

preface

When I read these notes for the first time, they were not yet in book form and I did not know the person who had written them. I was much younger then and I immediately identified with this man who had narrated his adventures in such a spontaneous manner. Of course, as I continued reading, I began to see more clearly who this person was and I was very happy to be his daughter.

It is not my aim to tell you anything of what you will discover in this reading, but I do not doubt that when you have finished the book you will want to go back to enjoy some passages again, either for the beauty of what they describe or because of the intensity of the feelings they convey.

There were moments when I literally took over Granado's place on the motorbike and clung to my dad's back, journeying with him over the mountains and around the lakes. I admit there were some occasions when I left him to himself, especially at those times he describes so graphically when he was doing things I would never talk about myself. When he does, however, he reveals yet again just how honest and unconventional he could be.

To tell you the truth, I should say that the more I read, the more in love I was with the boy my father had been. I do not know if you will share these sentiments with me, but while I was reading, I got to know the young Ernesto better: the Ernesto who left Argentina with his yearning for adventure and his dreams of the great deeds he would perform, and the young man who, as he discovered the reality of our continent, continued to mature as a human being and to develop as a social being.

Slowly we see how his dreams and ambitions changed. He grew increasingly aware of the pain of many others and he allowed it to become part of himself.

The young man who makes us smile at the beginning with his absurdities and his craziness, becomes before our eyes increasingly sensitive as he tells us about the complex indigenous world of Latin America, the poverty of its people and the exploitation to which they are submitted. In spite of it all, he never loses his sense of humor, but it becomes finer and more subtle.

My father, "*ese, el que fue*" (this man, the one who was), shows us a Latin America that few of us know about, describing its landscapes with words that color each image and reach into our senses, so that we too can see the things his eyes took in.

His prose is fresh. He uses words that allow us to hear sounds we have never heard before, infusing us with the surroundings that struck this romantic being with their beauty and their crudeness, yet he never loses his tenderness even as he becomes firmer in his revolutionary longing. In his consciousness the awareness grows that what poor people need is not so much his scientific knowledge as a physician, but rather his strength and persistence in trying to bring about social change that would enable them to live with the dignity that was taken from them and trampled on for centuries.

This young adventurer with his thirst for knowledge and his great capacity to love shows us how reality, if properly interpreted, can permeate a human being to the point of changing his or her way of thinking.

Read these notes of his that were written with so much love, eloquence and sincerity, these notes that more than anything else make me feel closer to my father. I hope you enjoy them and that you can join him on his journey.

If you ever have the opportunity to follow his footsteps in reality, you will discover with sadness that many things remain unchanged or are even worse, and this is a challenge for those of us who — like this young man who years later would become Che — are sensitive to the reality that so mistreats the most wretched among us, those of us who have a commitment to helping to create a world that is much more just.

I shall leave you now with the man I knew, the man I love intensely for the strength and tenderness he demonstrated in the way he lived.

Enjoy your reading! Ever onward!

Aleida Guevara March
July 2003

preface to the first edition

Ernesto Guevara's travel diaries, transcribed by Che's Personal Archive in Havana, recount the trials, vicissitudes and tremendous adventure of a young man's journey of discovery through Latin America. Ernesto began writing these diaries when, in December 1951, he set off with his friend Alberto Granado on their long-awaited trip from Buenos Aires, down the Atlantic coast of Argentina, across the Pampa, through the Andes and into Chile, and from Chile northward to Peru and Colombia and finally to Caracas.

These experiences were later rewritten by Ernesto himself as a narrative, offering the reader a deeper insight into Che's life, especially at a little known stage, and revealing details of his personality, his cultural background and his narrative skill — the genesis of a style which develops in his later works. The reader can also witness the extraordinary change which takes place in him as he discovers Latin America, gets right to its very heart and develops a growing sense of a Latin American identity which makes him a precursor of the new history of America.

Aleida March, 1993
Che's Personal Archive
Havana, Cuba

ernesto che guevara

One of *Time* magazine's "icons of the century," Ernesto Guevara de la Serna was born in Rosario, Argentina, on June 14, 1928. He made several trips around Latin America during and immediately after his studies at medical school in Buenos Aires, including his 1952 journey with Alberto Granado, on the unreliable Norton motorbike described in this travel diary.

He was already becoming involved in political activity and living in Guatemala when, in 1954, the elected government of Jacobo Arbenz was overthrown in a CIA-organized military operation. Ernesto escaped to Mexico, profoundly radicalized.

Following up on a contact made in Guatemala, Guevara sought out the group of exiled Cuban revolutionaries in Mexico City. In July 1955, he met Fidel Castro and immediately enlisted in the guerrilla expedition to overthrow Cuban dictator Fulgencio Batista. The Cubans nicknamed him "Che," a popular form of address in Argentina.

On November 25, 1956, Guevara set sail for Cuba aboard the yacht *Granma* as the doctor to the guerrilla group that began the revolutionary armed struggle in Cuba's Sierra Maestra mountains. Within several months, he became the first Rebel Army commander, though he continued ministering medically to wounded guerrilla fighters and captured soldiers from Batista's army.

In September 1958, Guevara played a decisive role in the military defeat of Batista after he and Camilo Cienfuegos led separate guerrilla columns westward from the Sierra Maestra.

After Batista fled on January 1, 1959, Guevara became a key leader of the new revolutionary government, first as head of the

Industrial Department of the National Institute of Agrarian Reform; then as president of the National Bank. In February 1961 he became minister of industry. He was also a central leader of the political organization that in 1965 became the Communist Party of Cuba.

Apart from these responsibilities, Guevara represented the Cuban revolutionary government around the world, heading numerous delegations and speaking at the United Nations and other international forums in Asia, Africa, Latin America and the socialist bloc countries. He earned a reputation as a passionate and articulate spokesperson for Third World peoples, most famously at the conference at Punta del Este in Uruguay, where he denounced U.S. President Kennedy's Alliance for Progress.

As had been his intention since joining the Cuban revolutionary movement, Guevara left Cuba in April 1965, initially to lead a guerrilla mission to support the revolutionary struggle in the Congo. He returned to Cuba secretly in December 1965, to prepare another guerrilla force for Bolivia. Arriving in Bolivia in November 1966, Guevara's plan was to challenge that country's military dictatorship and eventually to instigate a revolutionary movement that would extend throughout the continent of Latin America. He was wounded and captured by U.S.-trained and run Bolivian counter-insurgency troops on October 8, 1967. The following day he was murdered and his body hidden.

Che Guevara's remains were finally discovered in 1997 and returned to Cuba. A memorial was built at Santa Clara in central Cuba, where he had won a major military battle during the revolutionary war.

brief chronology of ernesto che guevara

1928

Ernesto Guevara is born on June 14 in Rosario, Argentina. He is the first child of middle-class parents Ernesto Guevara Lynch and Celia de la Serna.

1932

The Guevara family moves from Buenos Aires to Alta Gracia, a spa town near Córdoba, on account of Ernesto's chronic asthma. His asthma also prevents him from regular attendance at school until he is nine years old.

1948

Altering his initial plan to study engineering, Ernesto enrolls in medical school at the University of Buenos Aires, while holding a series of part-time jobs, including in an allergy treatment clinic.

1950

Ernesto sets out on a 4,500 kilometer trip around the north of Argentina on a motorized bicycle.

1951–52

In October 1951, Ernesto and his friend Alberto Granado decide on a plan to ride Alberto's motorbike (La Poderosa II — The Mighty One) to North America. Granado is a biochemist who had specialized in leprology and whose younger brothers had been Ernesto's school friends. They leave Córdoba in December, heading first to farewell Ernesto's family in Buenos Aires. The adventures experienced on this trip, written up by Ernesto during and after the journey, comprise this book, published first as *Notas de Viaje* (*Travel Notes* or *The Motorcycle Diaries*).

1953

Ernesto graduates as a doctor and almost immediately embarks on another journey around Latin America which takes in Bolivia, Peru, Ecuador, Panama, Costa Rica and Guatemala, where he meets Antonio (Ñico) López, a young Cuban revolutionary. In Bolivia, he is witness to the Bolivian Revolution. The account of these travels was first published as *Otra Vez* (*Once Again* or *On the Road Again*).

1954

Ernesto's political views are profoundly radicalized when in Guatemala he sees the overthrow by U.S.-backed forces of the democratically elected government of Jacobo Arbenz. He escapes to Mexico where he contacts the group of Cuban revolutionary exiles. In Mexico, he marries Peruvian Hilda Gadea with whom he has a daughter, Hildita.

1955

After meeting Fidel Castro, he agrees to join the group that is being organized to wage guerrilla war against the Batista dictatorship. Now called "Che" by the Cubans — a common nickname for Argentines — he sails as the troop's doctor on the yacht *Granma* in November 1956.

1956–58

Che soon demonstrates outstanding military ability and is promoted to the rank of commander in July 1957. In December 1958, he leads the Rebel Army to a decisive victory over Batista's forces at Santa Clara in central Cuba.

1959

In February, Che is declared a Cuban citizen in recognition of his contribution to the island's liberation. He marries Aleida March, with whom he has four children. In October, he is appointed head of the Industrial Department of the Institute of Agrarian Reform (INRA) and in November becomes president of the National Bank of Cuba where, with a gesture of disdain, he signs the new banknotes simply as "Che."

1960

Representing the revolutionary government, Che undertakes an extensive trip to the Soviet Union, the German Democratic Republic, Czechoslovakia, China and North Korea, signing several key trade agreements.

1961

Che is appointed head of the newly established Ministry of Industry. In August, he heads Cuba's delegation to the Organization of American States (OAS) at Punta del Este, Uruguay, where he denounces U.S. President Kennedy's Alliance for Progress.

1962

A fusion of Cuban revolutionary organizations takes place and Che is elected to the National Directorate. Che visits the Soviet Union for the second time.

1963

Che travels to Algeria which has just won independence from France under the government of Ahmed Ben Bella.

1964

Before heading off for an extensive trip around Africa, Che addresses the UN General Assembly in December.

1965

Che leads an international mission to the Congo to support the liberation movement founded by Patrice Lumumba. Responding to mounting speculation about Che's whereabouts, Fidel Castro reads Che's farewell letter to the Central Committee of the newly founded Cuban Communist Party. In December, Che returns to Cuba to prepare in secret for a new mission to Bolivia.

1966

Che arrives in Bolivia in November, in disguise.

1967

In April, Che's "Message to the Tricontinental" is published, calling for the creation of "two, three, many Vietnams." The same month, part of his guerrilla group becomes separated from the main detachment. On October 8, the remaining 17 guerrillas are ambushed and Che is wounded and captured. The following day he is murdered by Bolivian forces acting under instructions from Washington. His remains are buried in an unmarked grave along with the bodies of several other guerrilla fighters. **October 8** is designated the Day of the Heroic Guerrilla in Cuba.

1997

Che's remains are finally located in Bolivia and returned to Cuba where they are placed in a memorial at Santa Clara.

map of
the motorcycle diaries

Map not to scale.

itinerary of
the motorcycle diaries

ARGENTINA

1951

December   Córdoba to Buenos Aires

1952

January 4	Leave Buenos Aires
January 6	Villa Gesell
January 13	Miramar
January 14	Necochea
January 16–21	Bahía Blanca
January 22	En route to Choele Choel
January 25	Choele Choel
January 29	Piedra del Aguila
January 31	San Martín de los Andes
February 8	Nahuel Huapí
February 11	San Carlos de Bariloche

CHILE

February 14	Take the *Modesta Victoria* to Peulla
February 18	Temuco
February 21	Lautaro
February 27	Los Angeles
March 1	Santiago de Chile
March 7	Valparaíso
March 8–10	Aboard the *San Antonio*
March 11	Antofagasta
March 12	Baquedano
March 13–15	Chuquicamata
March 20	Iquique (and the Toco, La Rica Aventura and Prosperidad Nitrate Companies)
March 22	Arica

PERU

March 24	Tacna
March 25	Tarata
March 26	Puno
March 27	Sail on Lake Titicaca
March 28	Juliaca
March 30	Sicuani
March 31 – April 3	Cuzco
April 4–5	Machu Picchu
April 6–7	Cuzco
April 11	Abancay
April 13	Huancarama
April 14	Huambo
April 15	Huancarama
April 16–19	Andahuaylas
April 22–24	Ayacucho to Huancallo
April 25–26	La Merced
April 27	Between Oxapampa and San Ramón
April 28	San Ramón
April 30	Tarma
May 1–17	Lima
May 19	Cerro de Pasco
May 24	Pucallpa
May 25–31	Aboard *La Cenepa* sailing down Río Ucayali, a tributary of the Amazon
June 1–5	Iquitos
June 6–7	Aboard *El Cisne* sailing to the leper colony of San Pablo
June 8–20	San Pablo
June 21	Aboard the *Mambo-Tango* raft on the Amazon

COLOMBIA

June 23 – July 1	Leticia
July 2	Leave Leticia by plane
July 2–10	Bogotá
July 12–13	Cúcuta

VENEZUELA

July 14	San Cristóbal
July 16	Between Barquisimeto and Corona
July 17–26	Caracas, where Che and Alberto separate

UNITED STATES

| Late July | Miami |

ARGENTINA

| August | Che returns to his family in Córdoba |

introduction

If there is one hero in Latin America's struggle for liberation — stretching from Bolívar's[1] time until our own — who has attracted young people from Latin America and from all over the world, that hero is Ernesto Che Guevara. And though since his death he has become a modern myth, he has not yet been stripped of his youthful vitality. To the contrary, his mythic status has only served to heighten his youthfulness which, together with his daring and his purity, seem to constitute the secret essence of his charisma.

Becoming a myth, a symbol of so many scattered and fiercely held hopes, presupposes that such a character possesses a kind of gravity, a certain solemnity. It is good that this is so; historic utopia needs faces to embody it. But we shouldn't lose sight of the everyday nature of those human beings, who were children, teenagers and young people before they acquired the skills by which to guide us. It is not that I want to bury their exceptional natures in the common or familiar aspects of their lives, but that knowledge of those first, formative stages shows us the starting point for their later trajectories.

This is especially true in Che's case, whose account of this first trip he made with his friend Alberto Granado offers the young at heart such a close and cheerful, serious and at the same time ironic image of the young man, that we can almost glimpse his smile and hear his voice and asthmatic wheeze. He is young, like them, and he filled his whole life with youthfulness and matured his youth without diluting it.

This edition of *The Motorcycle Diaries*, the notes describing a journey made without hesitation, aboard the noisy motorcycle La Poderosa II (which gave out halfway, but only after transmitting to the adventure a joyous impulse we, too, receive), free as the wind, with the sole purpose of getting to know the world, is dedicated to people whose youth is not merely sequential, but is wholehearted and spiritual.

In the first pages, the young man who would become one of the genuine heroes of the 20th century cautions us, "This is not a story of incredible heroism." The word "heroism" rings out above the others, because we cannot read these pages without thinking of Che's future, an image of him in the Sierra Maestra, an image which reached perfection at Quebrada del Yuro in Bolivia.[2]

If this youthful adventure had not been prelude to his revolutionary formation, these pages would be different, and we would read them differently, though we cannot imagine how. Simply knowing that they are Che's — though he wrote them before becoming Che — makes us believe that he had a presentiment regarding the way they should be read. For example:

> The person who wrote these notes passed away the moment his feet touched Argentine soil. The person who reorganizes and polishes them, me, is no longer, at least I'm not the person I once was. All this wandering around "Our America with a capital A" has changed me more than I thought.

These pages are a testimony — a "photographic negative," as he also put it — of an experience that changed him, a first "departure" toward the outer world which, like his final departure, was Quixotic in its semi-unconscious style and, as for Quixote, had the same effect on the scope of his consciousness. This was the "spirit of a dreamer" experiencing an awakening.

In principle, and with the perfect logic of the unforeseeable, their journey was at first directed toward North America, as in fact it turned out to be: toward the "photographic negative" of North America that is South American poverty and helplessness, and toward real knowledge of what North America means for us.

"The enormity of our endeavor escaped us in those moments, all we could see was the dust on the road ahead and ourselves on the bike, devouring kilometers in the flight northward." Wasn't that "dust on the road" really, though without Che realizing it, the same dust José Martí[3] saw when he traveled from La Guaira to Caracas "in a common little coach"? Wasn't it the Quixotic dust in which the ghosts of American redemption appeared, "the natural cloud of dust that must rise when our terrible casing of chains falls to the ground"?[4] But Martí was coming from the north, and Che was traveling toward himself, catching only glimpses of his destiny, which we glimpse as well through his anecdotes and vignettes.

Comeback, the little dog with "aviator's impulses" Che presents to us so comically, leaping around the motorcycle from Villa Gesel to Miramar, reappears years later in the Sierra Maestra mountains as a puppy who must be strangled, because of its "hysterical howls" during an unsuccessful ambush laid in the hope of catching [Batista's notorious army colonel] Sánchez Mosquera. "With one last nervous twitch, the puppy stopped moving. There it lay, sprawled out, its little head spread over the twigs."[5] But, at the end of this incident from *Episodes of the Revolutionary War*, another dog appears lying in the hamlet of Mar Verde:

> Félix patted its head, and the dog looked at him. Félix returned the glance, and then he and I exchanged a guilty look. Suddenly everyone fell silent. An imperceptible stirring came over us, as the dog's meek yet roguish gaze seemed to contain a hint of reproach. There, in our presence, though observing us through the eyes of another dog, was the murdered puppy.

It was Comeback who had returned, living up to his name, reminding us also of what Ezequiel Martínez Estrada, our other great Argentine, said about José Martí's campaign diary:

> These emotions, these sensations, cannot be described or expressed in the language of poets and painters, musicians and mystics; they must be... absorbed without reply, as animals do with their contemplative and entranced eyes.[6]

A comparison of *Episodes of the Revolutionary War* with *The Motorcycle Diaries* shows us that, even though more than 10 years had passed, the latter was a literary model for the former. It contains the same moderation; the same candor; the same nimble freshness; exactly the same concept of moments used to provide unity for each brief chapter; and, of course, the same imperturbable steadiness that accepts both happy and tragic events without sharp inhalation or exhalation.

It isn't literary skill but fidelity to experience and narrative effectiveness that is sought. When both are attained, skill comes naturally, taking up its allotted place, neither blinding nor disturbing but making its contribution. Here, with little fumbling or hesitation, Che's style is already formed. The years would polish it, just as he himself polished his will with the pleasure of an artist, though not that of a wordsmith: a quiet shyness forced him not to dwell too much but to push on with the words toward the poetry of the naked image, which his minimal touch turned into reality. His "I—it-in-me" circle opens and closes continually without ever becoming dense, accommodating a style that prefers to remain hidden. The prose on the page sheds light, though does not drag on the imperceptible lightness of the narrative. It flows between description of feeling (in *Episodes*, "the determined murderer left a trail of burned huts, of sullen sadness...") and narrative accounts in which he searches for himself (in the *Diaries*, "Man, the measure of all things, speaks here through my mouth and narrates in my own language that which my eyes have seen") and sometimes even seems to be watching us.

What the eyes have seen, Che's colorful prose, paints objects as far as he can see and often, if the landscape permits it, with an intimate touch:

> The road snakes between the low foothills that sound the beginning of the great cordillera of the Andes, then descends steeply until it reaches an unattractive, miserable town, surrounded in sharp contrast by magnificent, densely wooded mountains.

The episode of the attempt at stealing wine, and others in ranks of the cheeky tradition, contains precious pearls of diction:

> The fact was, we were as broke as ever, retracing in our minds the smiles that had greeted my drunken antics, trying to find some trace of the irony with which we could identify the thief.

A sense of strangeness returns. In the chapter *Circular Exploration*: "As night fell it brought us a thousand strange noises and the sensation of walking into empty space with each step." In *Episodes*: "Then, in the middle of the ambush, an eerie moment of silence arose. When we went to gather the dead after the initial shooting, there was no one on the highway…" The imagery is fairly bursting with both the abundance and the silence of the visual world:

> The huge figure of a stag dashed like a quick breath across the stream and his body, silver by the light of the rising moon, disappeared into the undergrowth. This tremor of nature cut straight to our hearts. (*The Motorcycle Diaries*)

> [Fidel's] voice and presence in the woods, lit up by the torches, took on moving tones, and you could see that our leader changed the ideas of many people. (*Episodes*)

Though reference is made to [Fidel's] voice and tone, the scene seems silent to us, as if it has been witnessed from afar.

In these travel notes, several Quixotic or Chaplinesque episodes
— such as the already cited theft of the wine, the nocturnal pursuit
of the two young men "by a furious swarm of dancers," their enlist-
ment in a corps of Chilean firefighters, the delectable escapade of
the melons and their trail over the waves, and the enigma of the
impossible photo in a miserable hut on a hill near Caracas — are
wrapped in a similar silence.

La Poderosa's near to last stand is told with cinematographic
effect and we seem to be watching it all amid a film-like silence:

> I threw on the hand brake which, soldered ineptly, broke too.
> For some moments, I saw nothing more than the blurred shape
> of cattle flying past us on each side, while poor Poderosa gath-
> ered speed down the steep hill. By an absolute miracle we man-
> aged to graze only the leg of the last cow, but in the distance a
> river was screaming toward us with terrifying efficacy. I veered
> on to the side of the road and in the flash of an eye the bike
> mounted the two-meter bank, embedding us between two rocks,
> but we were unhurt.

These youthful adventures — veined with cheerfulness, humor and
frequently self-directed irony — seek the spirit of the landscape
rather than merely the scenery. That "spirit" was found in the sudden appearance of the deer: "We walked slowly so as not to disturb
the peace of the wild sanctuary with which we were now communing." Che writes with none of the sarcasm he dedicates to the topic
of religion: "Both [of us] assistants waited for Sunday [and the roast]
with a kind of religious devotion." So while being unbelievers, they
were able to feel the metaphorical presence of a "sanctuary" in nature, where they were in close rapport with its "spirit" — immediately reminding us of analogous images from the freethinking Martí,
such as this from his *Simple Verses*: "The bishop of Spain seeks /
Supports for his shrine. / On wild mountain peaks / The poplars
are mine."[7]

On March 7, 1952, in Valparaíso, they came face to face with injustice, whose victim was an asthmatic old woman, a customer in a small shop by the name of La Gioconda:

> The poor thing was in a pitiful state, breathing the acrid smell of concentrated sweat and dirty feet that filled her room, mixed with the dust from a couple of armchairs, the only luxury items in her house. On top of her asthma, she had a heart condition.

After completing a picture of total ruin, and further embittered by the animosity of the sick woman's family, Che — who felt helpless as a doctor and was approaching the awakening of conscience that would trigger his other, definitive vocation — wrote these memorable words:

> It is there, in the final moments, for people whose farthest horizon has always been tomorrow, that one comprehends the profound tragedy circumscribing the life of the proletariat the world over. In those dying eyes there is a submissive appeal for forgiveness and also, often, a desperate plea for consolation which is lost to the void, just as their body will soon be lost in the magnitude of the mystery surrounding us.

Unable to continue their journey any other way, the pair decided to stow away on a ship that would take them to Antofagasta, Chile. At that moment, they — or, at least, Che — did not see things so clearly:

> There (looking at the sea, leaning side by side on the railing of the *San Antonio*), we understood that our vocation, our true vocation, was to move for eternity along the roads and seas of the world. Always curious, looking into everything that came before our eyes, sniffing out each corner but only ever faintly — not setting down roots in any land or staying long enough to see the substratum of things; the outer limits would suffice.

The sea held a greater attraction than the voyagers' "road," because where land demands that even those in passing take root, the sea represents absolute freedom from all ties. "And now, I feel my great roots unearth, free, and…" The verse that heads the chapter on his liberation from Chichina says it all. All? Che tore up another root in the presence of the old asthmatic Chilean woman. And soon his chest would be stung again when he made friends with a married Chilean couple, communist workers who were harassed in Baquedano.

> The couple, numb with cold, in the desert night, huddling against each other in the desert night, were a living representation of the proletariat in any part of the world.

Like good sons of San Martín,[8] they shared their blankets with them.

> It was one of the coldest times in my life, but also one which made me feel a little more brotherly toward this strange, for me anyway, human species.

That strangeness, that deep separation and intrepid solitude in which he was still wrapped, is curious. There is nothing lonelier than adventure. Until he was filled with pity for the galley slaves and for the whipped child, Don Quixote was alone, surrounded by strangeness, by the craziness of the world around him. In his *Meditations on Quixote*, José Ortega y Gasset wrote, as the center of his reflections, "I am myself and my circumstances," which has usually been understood as the sum or symbiosis of two factors. It may also be understood as a dilemma in which the "I" or "myself" expresses those two factors as separated, distanced, though intensely related. This dilemma appeared in Che's memoirs of his first "departure," when he said:

> Although the blurred silhouette of the couple was nearly lost in the distance separating us, we could still see the man's singularly determined face and we remembered his straightforward invitation: "Come, comrades, let's eat together. I, too, am a tramp," which showed his underlying disdain for the parasitic nature he saw in our aimless traveling.

Whose was this secret disdain: the humble worker's or Che's? Or perhaps neither, but that the meeting "in the desert night," the sharing of the *mate*, bread, cheese and blankets, caused a spark which lit up a painful separation.

At any rate, we were in Chuquicamata, with the mine and the miner from the south:

> Cold efficiency and impotent resentment go hand in hand in the big mine, linked in spite of the hatred by a common necessity to live, on the one hand, and to speculate on the other…

An imposing suggestion appeared, and the leap to a kind of idea which would achieve its context, its possible meaning, years later in Cuba:

> …we will see whether some day, some miner will take up his pick in pleasure and go to poison his lungs with a conscious joy. They say that's what it's like over there, where the red blaze that now lights up the world comes from. So they say. I don't know.

In fact, in Cuba in 1964, Che would link these ideas with the words of the poet León Felipe (I don't know if Che was familiar with them when writing the lines above): "No one has yet been able to dig to the rhythm of the sun… no one has cut an ear of corn with love and grace."

> I quote these words because today we could tell that great, desperate poet to come now to Cuba; to see how human beings, after passing through all of the stages of capitalist alienation and after thinking of themselves as beasts of burden harnessed to the yoke of the exploiter, have rediscovered their path and have found their way back to play. Now, in our Cuba, work is acquiring a new meaning and is done with a new joy.[9]

Yet in March 1952, Che simply wrote, "we will see." The harsh lessons continued in the chapter *Chuquicamata*, named after the mining town that was "like a scene from a modern drama," and which he soberly described with a balance of impression, reflection and data. Its greatest lesson was "taught by the graveyards of the mines, containing only a small share of the immense number of people devoured by cave-ins, the silica and the hellish climate of the mountain." In his note of March 22, 1952, or some time later revising his notes, Che concluded: "The biggest effort Chile should make is to shake its uncomfortable Yankee friend from its back, a task that for the moment at least is colossal." The name Salvador Allende stops us in our tracks.

On the motorcycle, on trucks or in vans, on a ship or in a little Ford; sleeping in police stations, under the stars or in occasional shelters; Che struggling almost constantly with his asthma, the two friends crossed Argentina and Chile. They entered Peru on foot. The Peruvian Indians had a huge impact on them, just as the Mexican Indians had impressed Martí:

> These people who watch us walk through the streets of the town are a defeated race. Their stares are tame, almost fearful, and completely indifferent to the outside world. Some give the impression that they go on living only because it's a habit they cannot shake.

They come to the kingdom of defeated stone, Pachamama's kingdom, the Earth Mother who receives the spat-out "chewed coca-leaves instead of stones" with their accompanying "troubles." The center, or navel of the world, where Mama Ocllo dropped her golden wedge into the earth. The place Viracocha chose: Cuzco. And there, in the middle of the baroque procession of the Lord of the Earthquakes, "a brown Christ," they find an eternal reminder of the north which can only be seen from South America, its fatal and denouncing antithesis:

> Standing over the small frames of the Indians gathered to see the procession pass, the blond head of a North American can

occasionally be glimpsed, who, with his camera and sports shirt, seems to be (and in fact, actually is) a correspondent from another world...

The cathedral of Cuzco brought out the artist in Che, with such observations as this: "Gold doesn't have the gentle dignity of silver which becomes more charming as it ages, and so the cathedral seems to be decorated like an old woman with too much makeup." Of the many churches he visited, he was particularly struck by the lonely, disreputable and "pitiful image of the bell towers of the Church of Belén, toppled by the earthquake, lying like a dismembered animal on the hillside." But his most penetrating judgment of Peruvian colonial baroque is found in the lines of his sharply contrasting description of Lima's cathedral:

> There in Lima, the art has been stylized, with an almost effeminate touch: the cathedral towers are tall and graceful, maybe the most slender of all the cathedrals in the Spanish colonies. The lavishness of the woodwork in Cuzco has been left behind and taken up here in gold. The naves are light and airy, in contrast with those dark and hostile caverns of the Incan city. The paintings are also bright, almost joyous, and of schools more recent than the hermetic mestizos, who painted their saints with a dark and captive fury.

Their visit to Machu Picchu on April 5 served as the subject for a newspaper article that Che published in Panama on December 12, 1953, in which there is a careful gathering of data and historical information, and a didactic intention that was absent from his personal notes.

Something similar occurred in an article entitled "A Glance at the Banks of the Giant of Rivers," which was also published in Panama, on November 22, 1953, though in this Che placed greater emphasis on experience, describing his journey down the Amazon on a raft. The raft, humorously christened *Mambo-Tango* — so they wouldn't be accused of being fanatics about the latter — enabled

Che and Alberto, with a lot of hard work and danger, to learn about the harsh reality of the Amazonian Indians.

From the solitary heights of the "enigmatic stone blocks" to the debilitating neglect they witnessed on the banks of the Amazon, it was like traveling through a genetic map of the Americas. Celebrating his 24th birthday in the leper colony of San Pablo, Che spoke, in a style reminiscent of Bolívar and Martí: "We constitute a single mestizo race, which from Mexico to the Magellan Straits bears notable ethnographic similarities. And so, in an attempt to rid myself of the weight of small-minded provincialism, I propose a toast to Peru and to a United Latin America."

There was no hint of solemnity in these words; rather, pretending his words were merely rhetorical, he spoke with a confidence that placed them outside all convention: "My oratory offering was received with great applause." He did the same in a letter that he wrote to his mother from Bogotá on July 6, 1952, (included here to complete the description of his Colombian experiences), when he referred once again to his "Pan-American speech, which won great applause from the eminent, and eminently drunk, audience," and when he commented, with affectionate sarcasm, on Granado's own words of gratitude: "Alberto, who sees himself as Perón's natural heir, delivered such an impressive demagogic speech that our well-wishers were convulsed with laughter." But he spoke in a very different tone of the lepers and their lives, using moderation to try — in vain — to hide his own suffering. Writing about their departure from the San Pablo leper colony, Che said:

> That night an assembly of the colony's patients gave us a farewell serenade, with lots of local songs sung by a blind man. The orchestra was made up of a flute player, a guitarist and a *bandoneón* player with almost no fingers, and a "healthy" contingent helping out with saxophone, a guitar and some percussion. After that came the time for speeches, in which four patients spoke as well as they could, a little awkwardly. One of them froze, unable to

go on, until out of desperation he shouted, "Three cheers for the doctors!" Afterwards, Alberto thanked them warmly for their welcome...

Che described the scene in detail in the letter to his mother, ("the accordion player with no fingers on his right hand used little sticks tied to his wrist" and "almost all the others were hideously deformed, due to the nervous form of the disease"), trying unsuccessfully not to sadden her too much, comparing it with a "scene from a horror movie," but the tearing beauty of that farewell was clear:

> The patients cast off and to the sound of a folk tune the human cargo drifted away from shore; the faint light of their lanterns giving the people a ghostly quality.

From his notes on their experiences with the lepers, for whom they surely did much good, not only by treating them but also by playing soccer and talking with them in the spirit of unprejudiced, fraternal, intense humanity — explaining the lepers' immense gratitude — we can perceive the origins of the budding revolutionary in Che. I emphasize these words: "If there's anything that will make us seriously dedicate ourselves to leprosy, it will be the affection showed us by the sick we've met along the way." Impossible to imagine at the time how serious and deep that dedication would be, understanding "leprosy" to mean all of human misery.

Having read these notes, filled with so many contrasts and teachings, with so much comedy and tragedy, like life itself, and having commented — not exhaustively, but only as suggestions — I conclude with the joyous image of Che arriving in Caracas, wrapped in his traveling blanket, looking around at the Latin American panorama "while shouting all sorts of verses along to the roar of the truck."

I'll leave you with no further commentary, because, in its terrible, unadorned majesty, that exceptional final chapter *A Note in the Margin* neither needs nor tolerates it. In fact, I'm not sure whether this unfathomable "revelation" should be placed at the beginning or the end of these "diaries"; the revelation Che saw "printed in the night sky"; his own fate; waiting for "the great guiding spirit to cleave humanity into two antagonistic halves"; the Great Semí who, in Martí's view of Our America, would go "astride its condor, spreading the seed of the new America through the romantic nations of the continent and the sorrowful islands of the sea."[10] It is an inexorable chapter that, like a tragic flash of lightning, illuminates for us the "sacred space" in the depths of the soul of one who called himself "this small soldier of the 20th century." Of one who, in our invincible hope, always takes "to the road" again, shield on his arm and feeling "the ribs of Rocinante"[11] beneath his heels.

1   Simón Bolívar led several armed rebellions, helping to win independence from Spain for much of Latin America. His vision was for a federation of Spanish-speaking South American states.

2   The ravine in which Che's guerrilla unit was ambushed on October 8, 1967, and Che himself taken hostage. He was murdered the following day.

3   José Martí, Cuban national hero and noted poet, writer, speaker and journalist. Martí founded the Cuban Revolutionary Party in 1892 to fight Spanish rule and oppose U.S. neocolonialism. He launched the 1895 independence war and was killed in battle.

4   José Martí, *Obras completas* (Complete Works), Havana: Editorial Nacional de Cuba, 1963–73, vol.7, pp.289-90.

5   Ernesto Che Guevara, *Episodes of the Revolutionary War*, forthcoming from Ocean Press, 2004.

6   Ezequiel Martínez Estrada, *Martí revolucionario* (Martí the Revolutionary), Havana: Casa de las Américas, 1967, p.414, no.184.

7   José Martí, *Op. cit.*, vol.16, p.68.

8   José de San Martín, Argentine national hero who played a major role in winning independence from Spain for Argentina, Chile and Peru.

9   Ernesto Che Guevara, *Obras, 1957–67* (Works, 1957–67), Havana: Casa de las Américas, 1970, vol.II, p.333.

10 José Martí, *José Martí Reader*, Ocean Press, 1999, p.120.

11 Che Guevara, *Che Guevara Reader*, Ocean Press, 2003, p.384.

the motorcycle diaries

NOTES ON A LATIN AMERICAN JOURNEY

ENTENDÁMONOS
so we understand each other

This is not a story of incredible heroism, or merely the narrative of a cynic; at least I do not mean it to be. It is a glimpse of two lives that ran parallel for a time, with similar hopes and convergent dreams.

In nine months of a man's life he can think a lot of things, from the loftiest meditations on philosophy to the most desperate longing for a bowl of soup — in total accord with the state of his stomach. And if, at the same time, he's somewhat of an adventurer, he might live through episodes of interest to other people and his haphazard record might read something like these notes.

And so, the coin was thrown in the air, turning many times, landing sometimes heads and other times tails. Man, the measure of all things, speaks here through my mouth and narrates in my own language that which my eyes have seen. It is likely that out of 10 possible heads I have seen only one true tail, or vice versa. In fact it's probable, and there are no excuses, for these lips can only describe what these eyes actually see. Is it that our whole vision was never quite complete, that it was too transient or not always well-informed? Were we too uncompromising in our judgments? Okay, but this is how the typewriter interpreted those fleeting impulses raising my fingers to the keys, and those impulses have now died. Moreover, no one can be held responsible for them.

The person who wrote these notes passed away the moment his feet touched Argentine soil. The person who reorganizes and polishes them, me, is no longer, at least I'm not the person I once was. All this wandering around "Our America with a capital A" has changed me more than I thought.

In any photographic manual you'll come across the strikingly clear image of a landscape, apparently taken by night, in the light of a full moon. The secret behind this magical vision of "darkness at noon" is usually revealed in the accompanying text. Readers of this book will not be well versed about the sensitivity of my retina — I can hardly sense it myself. So they will not be able to check what is said against a photographic plate to discover at precisely what time each of my "pictures" was taken. What this means is that if I present you with an image and say, for instance, that it was taken at night, you can either believe me, or not; it matters little to me, since if you don't happen to know the scene I've "photographed" in my notes, it will be hard for you to find an alternative to the truth I'm about to tell. But I'll leave you now, with myself, the man I used to be...

PRÓDROMOS
forewarnings

It was a morning in October. Taking advantage of the holiday on the 17th I had gone to Córdoba.* We were at Alberto Granado's

*At the time a national holiday to commemorate Juan Perón's 1945 release from prison. General Perón was president of Argentina from 1946 to 1955 and from 1973 until his death in 1974.

place under the vine, drinking sweet *mate** and commenting on recent events in this "bitch of a life," tinkering with La Poderosa II.** Alberto was lamenting the fact that he had to quit his job at the leper colony in San Francisco del Chañar and about how poor his pay was now at the Hospital Español. I had also quit my job, but unlike Alberto I was very happy to leave. I was feeling uneasy, more than anything because having the spirit of a dreamer I was particularly jaded with medical school, hospitals and exams.

Along the roads of our daydream we reached remote countries, navigated tropical seas and traveled all through Asia. And suddenly, slipping in as if part of our fantasy, the question arose:

"Why don't we go to North America?"

"North America? But how?"

"On La Poderosa, man."

The trip was decided just like that, and it never erred from the basic principle laid down in that moment: improvisation. Alberto's brothers joined us in a round of *mate* as we sealed our pact never to give up until we had realized our dream. So began the monotonous business of chasing visas, certificates and documents, that is to say, of overcoming the many hurdles modern nations erect in the paths of would-be travelers. To save face, just in case, we decided to say we were going to Chile.

My most important mission before leaving was to take exams in as many subjects as possible; Alberto's to prepare the bike for the long journey, and to study and plan our route. The enormity of our endeavor escaped us in those moments; all we could see was the dust on the road ahead and ourselves on the bike, devouring kilometers in our flight northward.

*The Argentine national drink, a tea-like beverage made from the herb *mate*.
**Granado's Norton 500 motorcycle, literally "The Mighty One."

EL DESCUBRIMIENTO DEL ÓCEANO
the discovery of the ocean

The full moon is silhouetted against the sea, smothering the waves with silver reflections. Sitting on a dune, we watch the continuous ebb and flow, each with our distinct thoughts. For me, the sea has always been a confidant, a friend absorbing all it is told and never revealing those secrets; always giving the best advice — whose meaningful noises can be interpreted any way you choose. For Alberto, it is a new, strangely perturbing sight, and the intensity with which his eyes follow every wave building, swelling, then dying on the beach, reflects his amazement. Nearing 30, Alberto is seeing the Atlantic for the first time and is overwhelmed by this discovery that signifies an infinite number of paths to all ends of the earth. The fresh wind fills the senses with the power and mood of the sea; everything is transformed by its touch; even Comeback* gazes, his odd little nose aloft, at the silver ribbons unrolling before him several times a minute.

Comeback is both a symbol and a survivor: a symbol of the union demanding my return; a survivor of his own bad luck — two falls from the bike (in one of which he and his bag flew off the back), his persistent diarrhoea and even getting trampled by a horse.

We're in Villa Gesell, north of Mar del Plata, enjoying in his house my uncle's hospitality and reliving our first 1,200 kilometers — apparently the easiest, though they've already given us a healthy respect for distances. We have no idea whether or not we'll get there, but we do know the going will be hard — at least that's the impression we have at this stage. Alberto laughs at his minutely detailed plans for the trip, according to which we should be nearing

*The English nickname Ernesto has given to the little dog he's taking to Chichina, his girlfriend who is holidaying in Miramar.

the end when in reality we have only just begun.

We left Gesell stocked up on vegetables and tinned meat "donated" by my uncle. He asked us to send him a telegram from Bariloche — if we get there — so that with the number of the telegram he could buy a corresponding lottery ticket, which seemed a little optimistic to us. On cue, others taunted that the bike would be a good excuse to go jogging, etc., and though we have a firm resolve to prove them wrong, a natural apprehension keeps us from declaring our mutual confidence.

Along the coast road Comeback maintains his aviator's impulses, emerging unscathed from yet another head-on collision. The motorbike is very hard to control, with extra weight on a rack behind the center of gravity tending to lift the front wheel, and the slightest lapse in concentration sends us flying. We stop at a butcher store and buy some meat to grill and some milk for the dog, who won't even try it. I begin to worry more about the little animal's health than the money I'd forked out to pay for the milk. The meat turns out to be horse. It's unbearably sweet and we can't eat it. Fed up, I toss a piece away and amazingly, the dog wolfs it down in no time. I throw him another piece and the same thing happens. His regime of milk is lifted. In the middle of the uproar caused by Comeback's admirers I enter, here in Miramar, a...

...PARÉNTESIS AMOROSO
...lovesick pause

The intention of this diary is not really to recount those days in Miramar where Comeback found a new home, with one resident in particular to whom Comeback's name was directed. Our journey was suspended in that haven of indecision, subordinate to the words that give consent and create bonds.

Alberto saw the danger and was already imagining himself alone on the roads of America, though he never raised his voice. The struggle was between she and I. For a moment as I left, victorious, or so I thought, Otero Silva's lines rang in my ears:

> I heard splashing on the boat
> her bare feet
> And sensed in our faces
> the hungry dusk
> My heart swaying between her
> and the street, the road
> I don't know where I found the strength
> to free myself from her eyes
> to slip from her arms
> She stayed, crying through rain and glass
> clouded with grief and tears
> She stayed, unable to cry
> Wait! I will come
> walking with you.*

Yet afterwards I doubted whether driftwood has the right to say, "I win," when the tide throws it on to the beach it seeks. But that was later, and is of no interest to the present. The two days I'd planned stretched like elastic into eight and with the bittersweet taste of the goodbye mingling with my inveterate bad breath I finally felt myself lifted definitively away on the winds of adventure toward worlds I envisaged would be stranger than they were, into situations I imagined would be much more normal than they turned out to be.

I remember the day my friend the sea came to my defense — taking me from the limbo I was cursed with. The beach was deserted and a cold onshore wind was blowing. My head rested in the lap

*Miguel Otero Silva, left-wing Venezuelan poet and novelist, born in 1908.

tying me to this land, lulled by everything around. The entire universe drifted past rhythmically, obeying the impulses of my inner voice. Suddenly, a stronger gust of wind brought a different sea voice and I lifted my head in surprise, yet it seemed to be nothing, a false alarm. I lay back, returning once again in my dreams to the caressing lap. And then, for the last time, I heard the ocean's warning. Its vast and jarring rhythm hammered at the fortress within me and threatened its imposing serenity.

We became cold and left the beach, fleeing the disturbing presence which refused to leave me alone. The sea danced on the small stretch of beach, indifferent to its own eternal law and spawning its own note of caution, its warning. But a man in love (though Alberto used a more outrageous, less refined word) is in no condition to listen to such a call from nature; in the enormous belly of a Buick the bourgeois side of my universe was still under construction.

The first commandment for every good explorer is: An expedition has two points, the point of departure and the point of arrival. If your intention is to make the second theoretical point coincide with the actual point of arrival, don't think about the means — because the journey is a virtual space that finishes when it finishes, and there are as many means as there are different ways of "finishing." That is to say, the means are endless.

I remembered Alberto's suggestion: "The bracelet, or you're not who you think you are."

Chichina's hands disappeared into the hollow made by mine.

"Chichina, that bracelet... Can I take it to guide me and remind me of you?"

The poor girl! I know the gold didn't matter, despite what they say; her fingers as they held the bracelet were merely weighing up the love that made me ask for it. That is, at least, what I honestly think. Alberto says (with a certain mischievousness, it seems to me), that you don't need particularly sensitive fingers to weigh up the full 29 carats of my love.

HASTA ROMPER EL ULTIMO VÍNCULO
breaking the last tie

We left, stopping next in Necochea where an old university friend of Alberto's had his practise. We covered the distance easily in a morning, arriving just in time for a steak lunch, receiving a genial welcome from the friend and a not so genial welcome from his wife who spotted the danger in our resolutely bohemian ways.

"You have only one year left before you qualify as a doctor and yet you're going away? You have no idea when you'll be back? But why?"

We couldn't give precise answers to her desperate questions and this horrified her. She was courteous with us but her hostility was clear, despite the fact that she knew (at least I think she knew) ultimate victory was hers — her husband was beyond our "redemption."

We had visited in Mar del Plata a doctor friend of Alberto's who had joined the [Peronist] party, with all its consequent privileges. This doctor in Necochea remained faithful to his own — the Radicals — yet we, however, were as remote from one as from the other. Support for the Radicals was never a tenable political position for me and was also losing its significance for Alberto who had been quite close at one time with some of the leaders he respected.

When we climbed back on to the bike again, and after thanking the couple for our three days of the good life, we continued on to Bahía Blanca, feeling a little more alone but a good deal more free. Friends were also expecting us there, my friends this time, and they too offered us friendly and warm hospitality. Several days passed us by in this southern port, as we fixed the bike and wandered aimlessly around the city. These were the last days in which we did not have to think about money. Afterwards, a rigid diet of meat, polenta and bread would have to be followed strictly to stretch our meager finances. The taste of bread was now tinged with warning: "I won't be so easy to come by soon, old man," and we swallowed it with all the more enthusiasm. We wanted, like camels, to build our reserves for the journey that lay ahead.

The night before our departure I came down with a cough and quite a high temperature, and consequently we were a day late leaving Bahía Blanca. Finally, at three in the afternoon, we left under a blazing sun that by the time we reached the sand dunes around Médanos had become even hotter. The bike, with its badly distributed weight, kept bounding out of control, the wheels constantly spinning over. Alberto fought a painful battle with the sand and insists he won. The only certainty is that we found ourselves resting comfortably in the sand six times before we finally made it out on to the flat. We did, nevertheless, get out, and this is my *compañero's* main argument for claiming victory over Médanos.

From here I took over the controls, accelerating to make up for precious lost time. A fine sand covered part of a bend and — boom: the worst crash of the whole trip. Alberto emerged unscathed but my foot was trapped and scorched by the cylinder, leaving a disagreeable souvenir which lasted a long time because the wound wouldn't heal.

A heavy downpour forced us to seek shelter at a ranch but to reach it we had to get 300 meters up a muddy track, and we went flying another two times. Their welcome was magnificent but the sum total of our first experience on unsealed roads was alarming:

nine crashes in a single day. On camp beds, the only beds we'd know from now on, and lying beside La Poderosa, our snail-like dwelling, we still looked into the future with impatient joy. We seemed to breathe more freely, a lighter air, an air of adventure. Distant countries, heroic deeds and beautiful women spun around and around in our turbulent imaginations.

My tired eyes refused to sleep and in them a pair of green spots swirled, representing the world I had left for dead behind me and mocking the so-called liberation I sought. They harnessed their image to my extraordinary flight across the lands and seas of the world.

PARA LAS GRIPES, CAMA
for the flu, bed

The bike exhaled with boredom along the long accident-free road and we exhaled with fatigue. Driving on a gravel-covered road had transformed a pleasant jaunt into a heavy job. By nightfall, after an entire day of alternating turns at the controls, we were left with a greater desire to sleep than to continue with the effort to reach Choele Choel, a largish town where we had a chance at free lodging. So we stopped in Benjamín Zorrilla, settling down comfortably in a room at the railroad station. We slept, dead to the world.

We woke early the next morning, but when I went to collect water for our *mate* a weird sensation darted through my body, followed by a long shiver. Ten minutes later I was shaking uncontrollably like someone possessed. My quinine tablets made no difference, my head was like a drum hammering out strange rhythms, bizarre colors shifted shapelessly across the walls and some desperate heaving produced a green vomit. I spent the whole day like this, unable to eat, until by the evening I felt well enough to climb on the bike and, sleeping on Alberto's shoulder, we reached Choele Choel. There we visited Dr. Barrera, director of the little hospital and a member of parliament. He received us amiably, giving us a room to sleep in. He prescribed a course of penicillin and within four hours my temperature had lowered, but whenever we talked about leaving the doctor shook his head and said, "For the flu: bed." (This was his diagnosis, for want of a better one.) So we spent several days there, being cared for royally.

Alberto photographed me in my hospital gear. I made an impressive spectacle: gaunt, flushed, enormous eyes and a ridiculous beard whose shape didn't change much in all the months I wore it. It's a pity the photograph wasn't a good one; it was an acknowledgment of our changed circumstances and of the horizons we were seeking, free at last from "civilization."

One morning the doctor didn't shake his head in his usual way. That was enough. Within the hour we were gone, heading west toward our next destination — the lakes. The bike struggled, showing signs it was feeling the strain, especially in the bodywork which we constantly had to fix with Alberto's favored spare part — wire. He picked up this quote from somewhere, I don't know where, attributing it to Oscar Gálvez:* "When a piece of wire can replace a screw, give me the wire, it's safer." Our hands and our pants were unequivocal proof that we were with Gálvez, at least on the question of wire.

It was already night, yet we were trying to reach human habitation; we had no headlight and spending the night in the open didn't seem much like a pleasant idea. We were moving slowly, using a torch, when a strange noise rang out from the bike that we

*A champion Argentine rally driver.

couldn't identify. The torch didn't put out enough light to find the cause and we had no choice but to camp where we were. We settled down as best we could, erecting our tent and crawling into it, hoping to suffocate our hunger and thirst (for there was no water nearby and we had no meat) with some exhausted sleep. In no time, however, the light evening breeze became a violent wind, uprooting our tent and exposing us to the elements and the worsening cold. We had to tie the bike to a telephone pole and, throwing the tent over the bike for protection, we lay down behind it. The near hurricane prevented us from using our camp beds. In no way was it an enjoyable night, but sleep finally won out over the cold, the wind and everything else, and we woke at nine in the morning with the sun high above our heads.

By the light of day, we discovered that the infamous noise had been the front part of the bike frame breaking. We now had to fix it as best we could and find a town where we could weld the broken bar. Our friend, wire, solved the problem provisionally. We packed up and set off not knowing exactly how far we were from nearest habitation. Our surprise was great when, coming out of only the second bend, we saw a house. They received us very well, appeasing our hunger with exquisite roast lamb. From there we walked 20 kilometers to a place called Piedra del Aguila where we were able to weld the part, but by then it was so late we decided to spend the night in the mechanic's house.

Except for a couple of minor spills that didn't do the bike too much damage, we continued calmly on toward San Martín de los Andes. We were almost there and I was driving when we took our first real fall in the south, on a beautiful gravel bend, by a little bubbling stream. This time La Poderosa's bodywork was damaged enough to force us to stop and, worst of all, we found we had what we most dreaded: a punctured back tire. In order to mend it, we had to take off all the packs, undo the wire "securing" the rack, then struggle with the wheel cover which defied our pathetic crowbar. Changing the flat (lazily, I admit) lost us two hours. Late in the afternoon we stopped at a ranch whose owners, very welcoming Germans, had by rare coincidence put up an uncle of mine in the past, an inveterate old traveler whose example I was now emulating. They let us fish in the river flowing through the ranch. Alberto cast his line, and before he knew what was happening, he had jumping on the end of his hook an iridescent form glinting in the sunlight. It was a rainbow trout, a beautiful, tasty fish (even more so when baked and seasoned by our hunger). I prepared the fish while Alberto, enthusiastic from this first victory, cast his line again and again. Despite hours of trying he didn't get a single bite. By then it was dark and we had to spend the night in the farm laborers' kitchen.

At five in the morning the huge stove occupying the middle of this kind of kitchen was lit and the whole place filled with smoke. The farm laborers passed round their bitter *mate* and cast aspersions on our own "*mate* for girls," as they describe sweet *mate* in those parts. In general they didn't try to communicate with us, as is typical of the subjugated Araucanian race who maintain a deep suspicion of the white man who in the past has brought them so much misfortune and now continues to exploit them. They answered our questions about the land and their work by shrugging their shoulders and saying "don't know" or "maybe," quickly ending the conversation.

We were given the chance to stuff ourselves with cherries, so much so that by the time we were to move on to the plums I'd had enough and had to lie down to digest it all. Alberto ate some so as not to seem rude. Up the trees we ate avidly, as if we were racing each other to finish. One of the owner's sons looked on with a certain mistrust at these "doctors," disgustingly dressed and obviously famished, but he kept his mouth shut and let us eat to our idealistic hearts' content. It got to the point where we had to walk slowly so as to avoid stepping on our own stomachs.

We mended the kick-start and other minor problems and set off again for San Martín de los Andes where we arrived just before dark.

SAN MARTÍN DE LOS ANDES
san martín de los andes

The road snakes between the low foothills that sound the beginning of the great cordillera of the Andes, then descends steeply until it reaches an unattractive, miserable town, surrounded in sharp contrast by magnificent, densely wooded mountains. San Martín lies on the yellow-green slopes that melt into the blue depths of Laguna Lacar, a narrow tongue of water 35 meters wide and 500 kilometers long. The day it was "discovered" as a tourist haven the town's climate and transport difficulties were solved and its subsistence secured.

Our first attack on the local clinic completely failed but we were told to try the same tactic at the National Parks' offices. The superintendent of the park allowed us to stay in one of the tool sheds. The nightwatchman arrived, a huge, fat man weighing 140 kilos with a face as hard as nails, but he treated us very amiably, granting us permission to cook in his hut. That first night passed perfectly. We slept in the shed, content and warm on straw — certainly necessary in those parts where the nights are particularly cold.

We bought some beef and set off to walk along the shores of the lake. In the shade of the immense trees, where the wilderness had arrested the advance of civilization, we made plans to build a laboratory in this place, when we finished our trip. We imagined great windows that would take in the whole lake, winter blanketing the ground in white; the dinghy we would use to travel from one side to the other; catching fish from a little boat; everlasting excursions into the almost virgin forest.

Although often on our travels we longed to stay in the formidable places we visited, only the Amazon jungle called out to that sedentary part of ourselves as strongly as did this place.

I now know, by an almost fatalistic conformity with the facts, that my destiny is to travel, or perhaps it's better to say that traveling is our destiny, because Alberto is the same as me. Still, there are moments when I think with profound longing of those wonderful areas in our south. Perhaps one day, tired of circling the world, I'll return to Argentina and settle in the Andean lakes, if not indefinitely then at least for a pause while I shift from one understanding of the world to another.

At dusk we started back and it was dark before we arrived. We were pleasantly surprised to find that Don Pedro Olate, the night-watchman, had prepared a wonderful barbecue to treat us. We bought wine to return the gesture and ate like lions, just for a change. We were discussing how tasty the meat was and how soon we wouldn't be eating as extravagantly as we had done in Argentina, when Don Pedro told us he'd been asked to organize a barbecue for the drivers of a motor race taking place on the local track that coming Sunday. He wanted two helpers and offered us the job. "Mind that I can't pay you, but you can stock up on meat for later."

It seemed like a good idea and we accepted the jobs of first and second assistants to the "Granddaddy of the Southern Argentinean Barbecue."

Both assistants waited for Sunday with a kind of religious enthusiasm. At six in the morning on the day, we started our first job — loading wood on to a truck and taking it to the barbecue site — and we didn't stop work until 11 a.m. when the distinctive signal was given and everyone threw themselves voraciously on to the tasty ribs.

A very strange person was giving orders whom I addressed with the utmost respect as "Señora" any time I said a word, until one of my fellow workers said: "Hey kid, *che*, don't push Don Pendón too far, he'll get angry."

"Who's Don Pendón?" I asked, with the kind of gesture some uncultured kid would give. The answer, that Don Pendón was the Señora, left me cold, but not for long.

As always at barbecues, there was far too much meat for everyone, so we were given carte blanche to pursue our vocation as camels. We executed, furthermore, a carefully calculated plan. I pretended to get drunker and drunker and, with every apparent attack of nausea, I staggered off to the stream, a bottle of red wine hidden inside my leather jacket. After five attacks of this type we had the same number of liters of wine stored beneath the fronds of a willow, keeping cool in the water. When everything was over and the moment came to pack up the truck and return to town, I kept up my part, working reluctantly and bickering constantly with Don Pendón. To finish my performance I lay down flat on my back in the grass, utterly unable to take another step. Alberto, acting like a true friend, apologized for my behavior to the boss and stayed behind to look after me as the truck left. When the noise of the engine faded in the distance we jumped up and raced off like colts to the wine that would guarantee us several days of kingly consumption.

Alberto made it first and threw himself under the willow: his face was straight out of a comic film. Not a single bottle remained. Either my drunken state hadn't fooled anyone, or someone had seen me sneak off with the wine. The fact was, we were as broke as ever, retracing in our minds the smiles that had greeted my drunken antics, trying to find some trace of the irony with which we could identify the thief. To no avail. Lugging the chunk of bread and cheese we'd received and a few kilos of meat for the night, we had to walk back to town. We were well-fed and well-watered, but with our tails between our legs, not so much for the wine but for the fools they'd made of us. Words cannot describe it.

The following day was rainy and cold and we thought the race wouldn't go ahead. We were waiting for a break in the rain so we could go and cook some meat by the lake when we heard over the loudspeakers that the race was still on. In our role as barbecue assistants we passed free of charge through the entrance gates and, comfortably installed, watched a fairly good car race of the national drivers.

Just as we were thinking of moving on, discussing the best road to take, drinking *mate* in the doorway of our shed, a jeep arrived, carrying some of Alberto's friends from the distant and almost mythical Villa Concepción del Tío. We shared great and friendly hugs and went immediately to celebrate by filling our guts with frothy liquid, as is the dignified practise on such occasions.

They invited us to visit them in the town where they were working, Junín de los Andes, and so we went, lessening the bike's load by leaving our gear in the National Parks shed.

EXPLORACIÓN CIRCUNVALATORIA
circular exploration

Junín de los Andes, less fortunate than its lakeside brother, vegetates in a forgotten corner of civilization, unable to break free of the monotony of its stagnant life, despite attempts to invigorate the town by building the barracks where our friends were working. I say our friends, because in no time at all they were mine too.

We dedicated the first night to reminiscing about that distant past in Villa Concepción, our mood enhanced by seemingly unlimited bottles of red wine. My lack of training meant I had to abandon the match and, in honor of the real bed, I slept like a log.

We spent the next day fixing a few of the bike's problems in the workshop of the company where our friends worked. That night they gave us a magnificent farewell from Argentina: a beef and lamb barbecue, with bread and gravy and a superb salad. After several days of partying, we left, departing with many hugs on the road to Carrué, another lake in the region. The road is terrible and our poor bike snorted about in the sand as I tried to help it out of the dunes. The first five kilometers took us an hour and a half, but later the road improved and we arrived without any other hitches at Carrué Chico, a little blue-green lake surrounded by wildly forested hills, and then at Carrué Grande, a more expansive lake but sadly impossible to ride around on a bike because there is only a bridle path used by local smugglers to cross over to Chile.

We left the bike at the cabin of a park ranger who wasn't home, and took off to climb the peak facing the lake. It was nearing lunchtime and our supplies consisted only of a piece of cheese and some preserves. A duck passed, flying high over the lake. Alberto calculated the distance of the bird, the absence of the warden, the possibility of a fine, etc., and fired. By a masterful stroke of good luck (though not for the duck), the bird fell into the lake. A discussion immediately ensued as to who would go and get it. I lost and plunged in. It seemed that fingers of ice were gripping me all over my body, almost completely impeding my movement. Allergic as I am to the cold, those 20 meters there and back that I swam to retrieve what Alberto had shot down made me suffer like a Bedouin. Just as well that roast duck, flavored as usual with our hunger, is one exquisite dish.

Invigorated by lunch, we set off with enthusiasm on the climb.

From the start, however, we were joined by flies that circled us ceaselessly, biting when they got the chance. The climb was gruelling because we lacked appropriate equipment and experience, but some weary hours later we reached the summit. To our disappointment, there was no panoramic view to admire; neighboring mountains blocked everything. Whichever way we looked a higher peak was in the way. After some minutes of joking about in the patch of snow crowning the peak, we took to the task of descending, spurred on by the fact that darkness would soon be closing in. The first part was easy, but then the stream that was guiding our descent began to grow into a torrent with steep, smooth sides and slippery rocks that were difficult to walk on. We had to push our way through willows on the edge, finally reaching an area of thick and treacherous reeds. As night fell it brought us a thousand strange noises and the sensation of walking into empty space with each step. Alberto lost his goggles and my pants were reduced to rags. We arrived, finally, at the tree line and from there we took every step with infinite caution, because the dark was so complete and our sixth sense was heightened so much that we saw abysses every second moment.

After an eternity of trekking through deep mud we recognized the stream flowing out into the Carrué, and almost immediately the trees disappeared and we reached the flat. The huge figure of a stag dashed like a quick breath across the stream and his body, silver by the light of the rising moon, disappeared into the undergrowth. This tremor of nature cut straight to our hearts. We walked slowly so as not to disturb the peace of the wild sanctuary with which we were now communing.

We waded across the thread of water, whose touch against our ankles gave me a sharp reminder of those ice fingers I hate so much, and reached the shelter of the ranger's cabin. He was kind enough to offer us hot *mate* and sheepskins to sleep on till the following morning. It was 12:35 a.m.

We drove slowly on the way back, passing lakes of only a hybrid beauty compared to Carrué, and finally reached San Martín where Don Pendón gave us 10 pesos each for working at the barbecue. Then, we set off further south.

QUERIDA VIEJA
dear mama

January 1952
En route to Bariloche

Dear Mama,

Just as you have not heard from me, I've had no news from you and I'm worried. It would defeat the purpose of these few lines to tell you all that has happened to us; I'll just say that two days after leaving Bahía Blanca I fell ill with a temperature of 40 degrees which kept me in bed for a day. The following morning I managed to get up only to end up in the Choele Choel regional hospital where I was given a dose of a little-known drug, penicillin, and recovered four days later...

We reached San Martín de los Andes, using our usual resourcefulness to solve the thousand problems that plagued us along the way. San Martín de los Andes has a beautiful lake and is wonderfully set amid virgin forest. You must see it, I'm sure you'd find it worthwhile. Our faces are beginning to resemble the texture of Carborundum. Any house we come across that has a gardens, we seek food, lodging and whatever else is on offer. We ended up at the

Von Putnamers' ranch, they're friends of Jorge's, particularly one who's a Peronist, always drunk, and the best of the three. I was able to diagnose a tumor in the occipital zone that was probably of hydatic origin. We'll have to wait and see what happens. We will leave for Bariloche in two or three days and intend to travel at a leisurely pace. Send me a letter poste restante if it can arrive by February 10 or 12. Well, Mama, the next page I'm writing is for Chichina. Send lots of love to everyone and make sure you tell me whether or not Papi is in the south. A loving hug from your son.

POR EL CAMINO DE LOS SIETE LAGOS
the seven lakes road

We decided to go to Bariloche by the Seven Lakes road, named for the number of lakes the road skirts before reaching the town. We traveled the first few kilometers at La Poderosa's ever tranquil pace, without any serious mechanical upsets until, with nightfall chasing us down, we pulled the old broken headlight trick so we could sleep in a road laborer's hut, a handy ruse, because the cold that night was uncommonly harsh. It was so fiercely cold that a visitor soon appeared asking to borrow some blankets because he and his wife were camping by the edge of lake and were freezing. We went to share some *mate* with this stoical pair who for some time had been living beside the lakes with only a tent and the contents of their backpacks. They put us to shame.

We set off again, passing greatly varying lakes, all surrounded by ancient forest, the scent of wilderness caressing our nostrils. But curiously, the sight of a lake and a forest and a single solitary house with well-tended garden soon begins to grate. Seeing the landscape at this superficial level only captures its boring uniformity, not allowing you to immerse yourself in the spirit of the place; for that you must stop at least several days.

We finally reached the northern end of Lago Nahuel Huapí and slept on its banks, full and content after the enormous barbecue we had eaten. But when we hit the road again, we noticed a puncture in the back tire and from then began a tedious battle with the inner tube. Each time we patched up one side, the other side of the tube punctured, until we were all out of patches and were forced to spend the night where we were. An Austrian caretaker who had raced motorbikes as a young man gave us a place to stay, in an empty shed, caught between his desire to help fellow bikers in need and fear of his boss.

In his broken Spanish he told us that a puma was in the region. "And pumas are vicious, they're not afraid to attack people! They have huge blond manes…"

Attempting to close the door we found that it was like a stable door — only the lower half shut. I placed our revolver near my head in case the puma, whose shadow filled our thoughts, decided to pay an unannounced midnight visit. The day was just dawning when I awoke to the sound of claws scratching at the door. At my side, Alberto lay silent, full of dread. I had my hand tense on the cocked revolver. Two luminous eyes stared at me from the silhouetted trees. Like a cat, the eyes sprang forward and the black mass of the body materialized over the door.

It was pure instinct; the brakes of intelligence failed. My drive for self-preservation pulled the trigger. For a long moment, the thunder beat against and around the walls, stopping only when a lighted torch in the doorway began desperately shouting at us. But by that time in our timid silence we knew, or could at least guess, the reason for the caretaker's stentorian shouts and his wife's hysterical sobs as she threw herself over the dead body of Bobby — her nasty, ill-tempered dog.

Alberto went to Angostura to get the tire fixed and I thought I'd have to spend the night in the open, being unable to ask for a bed in a house where we were considered murderers. Luckily our bike was near another road laborer's hut and he let me sleep in the kitchen with a friend of his. At midnight I woke to the noise of rain and was going to get up to cover the bike with a tarpaulin. But before doing so, I decided to take a few puffs from my asthma inhaler, irritated by the sheepskin I was using for a pillow. As I inhaled, my sleeping companion woke up, hearing the puff. He made a sudden movement, then immediately fell silent. I sensed his body go rigid under his blankets, clutching a knife, holding his breath. With the experience of the previous night still fresh, I decided to remain where I was, for fear of being knifed, in case mirages were contagious in those parts.

We reached San Carlos de Bariloche by the evening of the next day and spent the night in the police station waiting for the *Modesta Victoria* to sail over toward the border with Chile.

Y YA SIENTO FLOTAR MI GRAN RAÍZ LIBRE Y DESNUDA... Y
and now, I feel my great roots unearth, free and...

In the kitchen of the police station we were sheltering from a storm unleashing its total fury outside. I read and reread the incredible letter. Just like that, all my dreams of home, bound up with those eyes that saw me off in Miramar, came crashing down for what seemed like no reason. A great exhaustion enveloped me and, half asleep, I listened to the lively conversation of a globetrotting prisoner as he concocted a thousand exotic brews, safe in the ignorance of his audience. I could make out his warm, seductive words while the faces surrounding him leaned closer so as better to hear his stories unfold.

As if through a distant fog I could see an American doctor we had met there in Bariloche nodding: "I think you'll get where you're heading, you've got guts. But I think you'll stay a while in Mexico. It's a wonderful country."

I suddenly felt myself flying off with the sailor to far-off lands, far away the current drama of my life. A feeling of profound unease came over me; I felt that I was incapable of feeling anything. I began to feel afraid for myself and started a tearful letter, but I couldn't write, it was hopeless to try. In the half-light that surrounded us, phantoms swirled around and around but "she" wouldn't appear. I still believed I loved her until this moment, when I realized I felt nothing.

I had to summon her back with my mind. I had to fight for her, she was mine, mine... I slept.

A gentle sun illuminated the new day, our day of departure, our farewell to Argentine soil. Carrying the bike on to the *Modesta Victoria* was not an easy task, but with patience we eventually did it. Getting it off again was equally as hard. Then, there we were in that tiny spot by the lake, pompously named Puerto Blest. A few kilometers on the road, three or four at most, and we were back on water, a dirty green lake this time, Laguna Frías.

A short voyage before finally reaching customs, then the Chilean immigration post on the other side of the cordillera — much lower at this latitude. There we crossed yet another lake fed by the waters of the Río Tronador that originate in the majestic volcano sharing the same name. This lake, Esmeralda, offered in contrast to the

Argentine lakes wonderful, temperate water, making the task of bathing very enjoyable and much more enticing. High in the cordillera at a place called Casa Pangue there is a lookout that affords a beautiful view over Chile. It is a kind of crossroads; at least in that moment it was for me. I was looking to the future, through the narrow band of Chile and to what lay beyond, turning the lines of the Otero Silva poem over in my mind.

OBJETOS CURIOSOS
curious objects

Water leaked from every pore of the big old tub carrying our bike. Daydreams took me soaring away while I maintained my rhythm at the pump. A doctor, returning from Peulla in the passenger launch that ran back and forth across Esmeralda, passed the hulking great contraption our bike was lashed to and where we were paying for both our and La Poderosa's passage with the sweat of our brows. A curious expression came across his face as he watched us struggling to keep the vessel afloat, naked and almost swimming in the oily pump-water.

We had met several doctors traveling down there to whom we lectured about leprology, embellishing a bit, provoking the admiration of our colleagues from the other side of the Andes. They were impressed because, since leprosy is not a problem in Chile, they didn't know the first thing about it or about lepers and confessed honestly that never in their lives had they even seen a leper. They told us about the distant leper colony on Easter Island where a small number of lepers were living; it was a delightful island, they said, and our scientific interests were excited.

This doctor generously offered us any help we might need, given the "very interesting journey" we were making. But in those happy days in the south of Chile, when our stomachs were still full and we were not yet totally brazen, we merely asked him for an introduction to the president of the Friends of Easter Island, who lived near them in Valparaíso. Of course, he was delighted.

The lake route ended in Petrohué where we said goodbye to everyone; but not before posing for some black Brazilian girls who placed us in their souvenir album for the southern Chile and for an environmentalist couple from who knows what European country, who noted our addresses ceremoniously so they could send us copies of the photos.

There was a character in the little town who wanted a station wagon driven to Osorno, where we were heading, and he asked me if I would do it. Alberto gave me a high-speed lesson in gear changes and I went off in all solemnity to assume my post. But rather cartoon-like I set off with hops and jerks behind Alberto who was riding the bike. Every corner was a torment: brake, clutch, first, second, help, *Mamaa*... The road wound through beautiful countryside, skirting Laguna Osorno, the volcano with the same name a sentinel above us. Unfortunately I was in no position along that accident-studded road to appreciate the landscape. The only accident, however, was suffered by a little pig that ran in front of the car while we were speeding down a hill, before I was fully practised in the art of braking and clutching.

We arrived in Osorno, we scrounged around in Osorno, we left Osorno and continued ever northward through the delightful Chilean countryside, divided into plots, every bit farmed, in stark contrast to our own arid south. The Chileans, exceedingly friendly people, were warm and welcoming wherever we went. Finally we arrived in the port of Valdivia, on a Sunday. Ambling around the city, we dropped into the local newspaper, the *Correo de Valdivia*, and they very kindly wrote an article about us. Valdivia was celebrating its fourth centenary and we dedicated our journey to the city in tribute to the great *conquistador* whose name the city bears. They persuaded us to write a letter to Molinas Luco, the mayor of Valparaíso, preparing him for our great Easter Island scam.

The harbor, overflowing with goods that were completely foreign to us, the market where they sold different foods, the typically Chilean wooden houses, the special clothes of the *guasos*,* were notably different from what we knew back home; there was something indigenously American, untouched by the exoticism invading our pampas. This may be because Anglo-Saxon immigrants in Chile do not mix, so preserving the purity of the indigenous race, which in our country is practically nonexistent.

But for all the customary and idiomatic differences distinguishing us from our thin brother of the Andes, there is one cry that seems international: "Give them water," the salutation greeting the sight of my calf-length trousers, not my personal taste but a fashion inherited from a generous, if short, friend.

LOS EXPERTOS
"the experts"

Chilean hospitality, as I never tire of saying, is one reason traveling in our neighboring country is so enjoyable. And we made the most

*Chilean peasants.

of it. I woke up gradually beneath the sheets, considering the value of a good bed and calculating the calorie content of the previous night's meal. I reviewed recent events in my mind: the treacherous puncture of La Poderosa's tire, which left us stranded in the rain and in the middle of nowhere; the generous help of Raúl, owner of the bed in which we were now sleeping; and the interview we gave to the paper *El Austral* in Temuco. Raúl was a veterinary student, not particularly studious it seemed, who had hoisted our poor old bike on to the truck he owned, bringing us to this quiet town in the middle of Chile. To be honest, there was probably a moment or two when our friend wished he'd never met us, since we caused him an uncomfortable night's sleep, but he only had himself to blame, bragging about the money he spent on women and inviting us for a night out at a "cabaret," which would be at his expense, of course. His invitation was the reason we prolonged our stay in the land of Pablo Neruda, and we became involved in a lively bragging session lasting for some time. In the end, of course, he came clean on that inevitable problem (a lack of funds), meaning we had to postpone our visit to that very interesting place of entertainment, though in compensation he gave us bed and board. So at one in the morning there we were, feeling very self-satisfied and devouring everything on the table, quite a lot really, plus some more that arrived later. Then we appropriated our host's bed since because his father was being transferred to Santiago there was not much furniture left in the house.

Alberto, unmovable, was resisting the morning sun's attempt to disturb his deep sleep, while I dressed slowly, a task we didn't find particularly difficult because the difference between our night wear and day wear was made up, generally, of shoes. The newspaper flaunted a generous number of pages, very much in contrast to our poor and stunted dailies, but I wasn't interested in anything besides one piece of local news I found in large type in section two:

TWO ARGENTINE LEPROSY EXPERTS TOUR
LATIN AMERICA BY MOTORCYCLE

And then in smaller type:

THEY ARE IN TEMUCO AND WANT TO VISIT RAPA-NUI

This was the epitome of our audacity. Us, experts, key figures in the field of leprology in the Americas, with vast experience, having treated 3,000 patients, familiar with the most important leprosy centers of the continent and researchers into the sanitary conditions of those same centers, had consented to visit this picturesque, melancholy little town. We supposed they would fully appreciate our respect for the town, but we didn't really know. Soon the whole family was gathered around the article and all other items in the paper became objects of Olympian contempt. And so, like this, basking in their admiration, we said goodbye to those people we remember nothing about, not even their names.

We had asked permission to leave the bike in the garage of a man who lived on the outskirts of town and we made our way there, no longer a pair of more or less likable vagrants with a bike in tow; no, we were now "The Experts," and we were treated accordingly. We spent the whole day fixing and conditioning the bike while every now and then a dark-skinned maid would arrive with little snacks. At five o'clock, after a delicious afternoon tea prepared by our host, we said goodbye to Temuco and headed north.

LAS DIFICULTADES AUMENTAN
the difficulties intensify

Our departure from Temuco went as normal until, on the road out of town, we noticed the back tire was punctured and we had to stop and fix it. We worked energetically but no sooner had we put the spare on we saw it was losing air; it too was punctured. It seemed we would have to spend the night out in the open as there was no question of repairing it at that time of night. But we weren't just anybody now, we were The Experts; and we soon found a railroad worker who took us to his house where we were treated like kings.

Early next morning we took the inner tubes and tire to the garage to remove some bits of metal that had become embedded, and to patch the tire again. It was close to nightfall when we left, but not before accepting an invitation to a typical Chilean meal: tripe and another similar dish, all very spicy, washed down with a delicious rough wine. As usual, Chilean hospitality wiped us out.

Of course we didn't get much further, and less than 80 kilometers on we stopped to sleep in the house of a park ranger who was hoping for a tip. Because it never arrived he refused us breakfast the following day, so we set off in bad humor intending to light a small fire and make some *mate* as soon as we'd done a few kilometers. We'd gone a little way and I was looking out for a good place to stop when, with no warning at all, the bike took a sharp twist sideways sending us flying to the ground. Alberto and I, unharmed, examined the bike — finding one of the steering columns broken and, most seriously, the gearbox smashed. It was impossible to go on. The only thing to do was wait patiently for an accommodating truck to take us as far as the next town.

A car going in the opposite direction stopped and its occupants got out to see what had happened and to offer their services. They told us they would do everything possible to help, with whatever two scientists like ourselves needed.

"Do you know, I recognized you straight away from the photo in the paper," one of them said.

But we had nothing to ask of them, except for a truck going the other way. We thanked them and settled down for the usual *mate* when the owner of a nearby shack came over and invited us in to his home. We downed a couple of liters in his kitchen. There we met with his *charango*, a musical instrument made with three or four wires some two meters in length stretched tightly across two empty tins fixed to a board. The musician uses a kind of metal knuckle-duster with which he plucks the wires producing a sound like a toy guitar. Around 12 a van came along whose driver, after much pleading, agreed to take us to the next town, Lautaro.

We found a space in the best garage in the area and someone who would be able to do the soldering, a short and friendly boy called Luna who once or twice took us home for lunch. We divided our time between working on the bike and scrounging something to eat in the homes of the many curiosity seekers who came to see us at the garage. Next door was a German family, or one of German origin, who treated us handsomely. We slept in the local barracks.

The bike was more or less fixed and we had decided to leave the following day, so we thought we'd throw caution to the wind with some new pals who invited us for a few drinks. Chilean wine is great and I was drinking it unbelievably quickly, so much so that by the time we went on to the village dance I felt ready to take on the world. The evening progressed pleasantly as we kept filling our bellies and our heads with wine. One of the particularly friendly mechanics from the garage asked me to dance with his wife because he'd been mixing his drinks and was not feeling very well. His wife was hot and clearly in the mood and, full of Chilean wine, I took her by the hand and tried to steer her outside. She followed me meekly but then noticed her husband watching us and told me she would stay behind. I was in no state to listen to reason and we began to argue in the middle of the dance floor. I started pulling her toward one of the doors, while everybody was watching, and then she tried to kick me, and as I was pulling her she lost her balance and fell crashing to the floor.

Running back toward the village, pursued by a furious swarm of dancers, Alberto loudly mourned the loss of the wine her husband might have bought us.

LA PODEROSA II TERMINA SU GIRA
la poderosa II's final tour

We rose early to put the finishing touches on the bike and to flee what was no longer a very hospitable place for us, but only after accepting a final invitation to lunch from the family who lived next to the garage.

Due to a premonition, Alberto didn't want to drive, so I sat up front though we only did a few kilometers before stopping to fix the failing gearbox. A little further on, as we rounded a tight curve at a good speed, the screw came off the back brake, a cow's head appeared around the bend, then many, many more of them, and I threw on the hand brake which, soldered ineptly, broke too. For some moments I saw nothing more than the blurred shape of cattle flying past us on each side, while poor Poderosa gathered speed down the steep hill. By an absolute miracle we managed to graze only the leg of the last cow, but in the distance a river was screaming toward us with terrifying efficacy. I veered on to the side of the road and in the flash of an eye the bike mounted the two-meter bank, embedding us between two rocks, but we were unhurt.

Ever aided by the letter of recommendation from the "press," we were put up by some Germans who treated us very well. During the night I had a bad case of the runs and, being ashamed to leave a souvenir in the pot under my bed, I climbed out on to the window ledge and gave up all of my pain to the night and blackness beyond. The next morning I looked out to see the effect and saw that two meters below lay a big sheet of tin where they were sun-drying their peaches; the added spectacle was impressive. We beat it from there fast.

Although at first glance the accident seemed to be of little importance, it quickly became clear we had underestimated the damage. The bike acted strangely every time it had to climb uphill. On the ascent to Malleco, where there is a railroad bridge considered by Chileans to be the highest in the Americas, the bike packed it in and we wasted the whole day waiting for some charitable soul (embodied in the shape of a truck) to take us to the top. We slept in the town of Cullipulli, after gaining the hoped-for lift, and left early, fearing impending catastrophe. On the first steep hill, one of many on that road, La Poderosa finally gave up the ghost. A truck took us to Los Angeles where we left her in the fire station and slept at the house of a Chilean army lieutenant who seemed very thankful for the way he'd been treated in our country Argentina and couldn't do enough to please us. It was our last day as "motorized bums"; the next stage seemed set to be more difficult, as "bums without wheels."

BOMBEROS VOLUNTARIOS, HOMBRES DE TRABAJO Y OTRAS YERBAS
firefighters, workers and other matters

As far as I know there are no non-volunteer fire brigades in Chile, but even so it's a very good service because captaining a brigade is a sought-after honor for the most able men in the towns or districts where they operate. And don't believe it's only a job in theory: in the south of the country at least, fires occur with astonishing frequency. I'm not sure what the major contributing factor is, whether it's because most buildings are constructed with wood, or because the cultural level of the people is quite low and they do not have much education, or some other factor, or all of them put together. What's certain is that in the three days we stayed at the fire station there were two big fires and one small one (though I'm not suggesting this was average, just stating the facts.)

I've forgotten to explain that after spending the night at the lieutenant's house, we decided to move to the fire station, lured by the charms of the caretaker's three daughters, exponents of the grace of Chilean women who, ugly or beautiful, have a certain spontaneity and freshness that captivates immediately. But I'm drifting from my point... They gave us a room where we set up our camp beds and fell into them with our habitual sleep of the dead, meaning we didn't hear the sirens. The volunteers on duty had no idea we were there and rushed off with their fire engines while we slept on until mid-morning, when we learned what had happened. We exacted promises from them to include us in the party for the next fire. We had found a truck that in two days would take us and the bike to Santiago for a low price, on condition we helped them with the load of furniture they were moving.

We made a very popular pair, with our abundant supply of conversation for the volunteers and the caretaker's daughters, and the days in Los Angeles flew by. In my eyes, constantly ordering and pencilling in the past, the symbolic representation of the town will always be the furious flames of a fire. It was the last day of our stay and after numerous toasts expressing the beautiful sentiments of our goodbyes, we had curled up in our blankets and gone to sleep. The much-awaited siren tore through the night, calling and waking the volunteers on duty, tearing also through Alberto's bed from which he sprang far too quickly. Soon we had taken our positions with the necessary gravity in the fire engine "Chile-España,"* which left the station at a breakneck speed, the long whine of its alarm that alarmed nobody, too often heard to constitute much of a novelty.

As each surge of water fell on to its flaming skeleton, the wood and adobe house shook. The acrid smoke of the burnt wood stood firm against the stoical work of the firefighters who, between fits of laughter, protected neighboring houses with jets of water or by other means. The flames hadn't reached a small part of the house and from there came the whimper of a cat who, terrorized by the fire, just meowed and meowed and refused to escape through the small space left. Alberto saw the danger, and measuring it with one quick look, leapt agilely over the 20 centimeters of flame saving the little endangered life for its owners. Receiving effusive congratulations for his unrivalled heroism, his eyes shone with pleasure from beneath the huge helmet he had borrowed.

But everything comes to an end, and Los Angeles gave us its final goodbye. Little Che and Big Che (Alberto and I) solemnly shook the last friendly hands as the truck began its journey to Santiago, carrying on its powerful back the corpse of La Poderosa II.

On a Sunday we arrived in Santiago and as our first measure we went directly to the Austin garage. We had a letter of introduction to the owner but were unhappily surprised to find that it was

*Almost all Chilean fire brigades have a sister city or country.

closed. In the end we got the caretaker to accept the bike, and went off to pay for part of the trip with the sweat of our brows.

Our job as removalists had different stages: the first, particularly interesting, consisted of consuming two kilos of grapes each in record time, assisted by the absence of the house owners; the second, their arrival and subsequently some heavy work; the third, Alberto's discovery that the truck driver's colleague had an overactive ego, especially with regard to his body; the poor guy won all the bets we made with him by carrying more furniture than both us and the owner combined (the latter played the fool with barbaric ease).

We'd managed to track down our consul who finally turned up at what served as an office, stone-faced (fair enough considering it was a Sunday), and he let us sleep on the patio. After a caustic diatribe regarding our duties as citizens, etc., he topped off his generosity by offering us 200 *pesos* which we, taking righteous offense, refused. If he'd offered it three months later, it would've been a different story. What a save!

Santiago has more or less the same feel as Córdoba. Though its daily pace is much faster and its traffic considerably heavier, its buildings, the nature of its streets, its weather and even the faces of its people, reminded us of our own Mediterranean city. We couldn't get to know the city well because we were there only a few days and were pressed for time with the many things we had to sort out before embarking once again.

The Peruvian consul refused to issue us visas without a letter from his Argentine counterpart, which the latter refused to give, saying the bike probably wouldn't get us there and we'd end up asking the embassy for help (the little angel was ignorant of the fact that the bike was already finished), but he finally relented and they gave us the visas for Peru, at a fee of 400 Chilean *pesos*, a lot of cash for us. In those days the Suquía water polo team from Córdoba was visiting Santiago. Many of the guys were friends of ours, so we paid them a courtesy call while they were playing a match and got ourselves invited to one of those Chilean-style meals that go something like: "have some ham, try some cheese, drink a little more wine," and that you stand up from — if you can — straining all the thorax muscles in your body. The following day we climbed up Santa Lucía, a rocky formation in the center of the city with its own particular history, and were peacefully performing the task of photographing the city when a convoy of Suquía members arrived, led by some good lookers from the host club. The poor guys were embarrassed enough — unsure of whether to introduce us to these "distinguished ladies of Chilean society," as in the end they did, or play dumb and pretend not to know us (remember our unorthodox attire). But they managed the tight spot as skilfully as possible and were very friendly — as friendly as people could be from worlds as different as theirs and ours at that particular moment in our lives.

The big day arrived at last and two tears ploughed symbolically down Alberto's cheeks. With one last goodbye to La Poderosa, left behind in the garage, we began our journey to Valparaíso. We set off along a magnificent mountain road, the most beautiful civilization could offer compared to the real natural wonders (undamaged by human hands, that is), in a truck bearing the heavy weight of us freeloaders.

LA SONRISA DE LA GIOCONDA
la gioconda's smile

We had come to a new phase in our adventure. We were used to calling idle attention to ourselves with our strange dress and the prosaic figure of La Poderosa II, whose asthmatic wheezing aroused pity in our hosts. To a certain extent we had been knights of the road; we belonged to that long-standing "wandering aristocracy" and had calling cards with our impeccable and impressive titles. No longer. Now we were just two hitchhikers with backpacks, and with all the grime of the road stuck to our overalls, shadows of our former aristocratic selves.

The truck driver had left us at the upper edge of the city, at its entrance, and with weary steps we dragged our packs down the streets, followed by the amused or indifferent glances of onlookers. In the distance the harbor radiated with the tempting glimmer of its boats, while the sea, black and inviting, cried out to us — its gray smell dilating our nostrils. We bought bread — which seemed so expensive at the time though it became cheaper as we ventured further north — and kept walking downhill. Alberto wore his exhaustion obviously, and although I tried not to show it I was just as tired. So when we found a truck stop we assaulted the attendant with our tragic faces, relating in florid detail the hardships we had suffered on the long hard road from Santiago. He let us sleep on some wooden planks, in the company of some parasites whose name ends in *hominis*, but at least we had a roof over our heads.

We set about sleeping with determination. News of our arrival, however, reached the ears of a fellow-countryman installed in a cheap restaurant next to the trailer park, and he wanted to meet us. To meet in Chile signifies a certain hospitality and neither of us was in a position to turn down this manna from heaven. Our compatriot proved to be profoundly imbued with the spirit of the sisterland and consequently was fantastically drunk. It was a long time since I'd eaten fish, and the wine was so delicious, and our host so attentive ... Anyway, we ate well and he invited us to his house the following day.

La Gioconda threw open its doors early and we brewed our *mate*, chatting with the owner who was very interested in our journey.

After that, we went to explore the city. Valparaíso is very picturesque, built to the edge of the beach and overlooking a large bay.
As it grew it clambered up the hills that sweep down to their deaths
in the sea. The madhouse museum beauty of its strange corruga-
ted-iron architecture, arranged on a series of tiers linked by winding
flights of stairs and funiculars, is heightened by the contrast of
diversely colored houses blending with the leaden blue of the bay.
As if patiently dissecting, we pry into dirty stairways and dark recesses, talking to the swarms of beggars; we plumb the city's depths,
the miasmas that draw us in. Our distended nostrils inhale the
poverty with sadistic intensity.

We visited the ships down at the docks to see if any were going
to Easter Island but the news was disheartening: it would be six
months before any boat was going there. We collected some vague
details about flights that left once a month.

Easter Island! The imagination stops in its ascending flight to
turn somersaults at the very thought: "Over there, having a white
'boyfriend' is an honor"; "Work? Ha! the women do everything —
you just eat, sleep and keep them content." This marvellous place
where the weather is perfect, the women are perfect, the food perfect,
the work perfect (in its beatific nonexistence). What does it matter
if we stay there a year; who cares about studying, work, family, etc.
In a shop window a giant crayfish winks at us, and from his bed
of lettuce his whole body tells us, "I'm from Easter Island, where
the weather is perfect, the women are perfect..."

In the doorway of La Gioconda we were waiting patiently for
our compatriot to show up, who gave no sign of appearing, when
the owner invited us in out of the sun and treated us to one of his
magnificent lunches of fried fish and watery soup. We never heard
from the Argentine again throughout our stay in Valparaíso, but
we became great friends with the owner of the bar. He was a strange
sort of guy, indolent and enormously generous to all the riff raff
who turned up, though he made normal customers pay colossal

prices for the paltry cuisine he sold in his place. We didn't pay a cent the whole time we were there and he lavished hospitality on us. "Today it's your turn, tomorrow it'll be mine" was his favorite saying; not very original but very effective.

We tried to contact the doctors from Petrohué, but being back at work with no time to spare, they never agreed to meet us formally. At least we knew more or less where they were. In the afternoon we went our separate ways: while Alberto followed up the doctors, I went to see an old woman with asthma, a customer at La Gioconda. The poor thing was in a pitiful state, breathing the acrid smell of concentrated sweat and dirty feet that filled her room, mixed with the dust from a couple of armchairs, the only luxury items in her house. On top of her asthma, she had a heart condition. It is at times like this, when a doctor is conscious of his complete powerlessness, that he longs for change: a change to prevent the injustice of a system in which only a month ago this poor woman was still earning her living as a waitress, wheezing and panting but facing life with dignity. In circumstances like this, individuals in poor families who can't pay their way become surrounded by an atmosphere of barely disguised acrimony; they stop being father, mother, sister or brother and become a purely negative factor in the struggle for life and, consequently, a source of bitterness for the healthy members of the community who resent their illness as if it were a personal insult to those who have to support them. It is there, in the final moments, for people whose farthest horizon has always been tomorrow, that one comprehends the profound tragedy circumscribing the life of the proletariat the world over. In those dying eyes there is a submissive appeal for forgiveness and also, often, a desperate plea for consolation which is lost to the void, just as their body will soon be lost in the magnitude of mystery surrounding us. How long this present order, based on an absurd idea of caste, will last is not within my means to answer, but it's time that those who govern spent less time publicizing their own virtues and more money, much more money, funding socially useful works.

There isn't much I can do for the sick woman. I simply advise her to improve her diet and prescribe a diuretic and some asthma pills. I have a few Dramamine tablets left and I give them to her. When I leave, I am followed by the fawning words of the old woman and the family's indifferent gaze.

Alberto had tracked down the doctor. At nine the following morning we had to be at the hospital. Meanwhile, in La Gioconda's filthy room which serves as kitchen, restaurant, laundry, dining room and piss-house for cats and dogs, a miscellaneous collection of people were meeting: the owner, with his basic life philosophy; Doña Carolina, a deaf and helpful old dear who left our *mate* kettle as good as new; a drunk, feeble-minded Mapuche* man who looked like a criminal; two more or less normal customers; and the queen of the gathering Doña Rosita, who was quite crazy. The conversation focused on a macabre event Rosita had witnessed; it appeared she alone had seen a man with a large knife thrashing her poor neighbor.

"Was your neighbor screaming, Doña Rosita?"

"Of course she was screaming, who wouldn't! He was skinning her alive! That's not all. Afterwards, he took her down to the sea and dragged her to the water's edge so the sea would take her away. Oh, to hear that woman scream, señor, scared the living daylight out of me, you should have seen it!"

"Why didn't you tell the police, Rosita?"

"Oh, what for? Don't you remember when your cousin was beat up? Well, I went to report it and they told me I was crazy, that if I didn't stop inventing things they'd lock me up, imagine that. No, I wouldn't tell that lot anything!"

The conversation turned to the "messenger from God," a local man who uses the powers God has given him to cure deafness, dumbness, paralysis, etc., passing the collection plate around after-

Mapuches are an indigenous people of Chile.

wards. The business seems no worse than any other, and though the pamphlets are extraordinary, so is people's gullibility. But that's how it is, and they continued to make fun of the things Doña Rosita saw with all the conviction in the world.

The reception from the doctors wasn't over-friendly, but we gained our objective: they gave us an introduction to Molinas Luco, mayor of Valparaíso. We took our leave with all the required formality and went to the town hall. Our dazed and exhausted expressions didn't impact favorably on the man at the desk, but he'd received orders to let us in.

The secretary showed us a copy of a letter written in response to ours, explaining that our project was impossible since the only ship to Easter Island had left and that there wouldn't be another ship leaving within the year. We were ushered into the sumptuous office of Dr. Molinas Luco, who received us amicably. He gave the impression, however, of acting out a scene in a play, taking a lot of care to pronounce each word perfectly. He became enthusiastic only when talking about Easter Island, which he had wrested from the English by proving it belonged to Chile. He recommended we keep up with events and said he would take us the following year. "I may not be in this office, but I am still president of the Friends of Easter Island Society," he said, a tacit confession of González Videla's impending electoral defeat. As we left, the man at the desk told us to take our dog with us, and to our amazement showed us a puppy that had done its business on the lobby carpet and was gnawing at a chair leg. The dog had probably followed us, attracted by our hobo appearance, and the doorman imagined it was just another accessory of our eccentric attire. Anyway, the poor animal, robbed of the bond linking him to us, got a good kick up the ass and was thrown out howling. Still, it was always consoling to know that some living thing's well-being depended on our protection.

By this time we were determined that traveling by sea we could avoid the desert in northern Chile, and we fronted up to the shipping companies requesting free passage to any of the northern ports. The captain at one of them promised to take us if we could arrange permission from the maritime authorities to work for our passage. The reply, of course, was negative and we found ourselves back at square one. In that split second, Alberto made a heroic decision, which went something like this: we would sneak on to the boat and hide away in the hold. For our best chance we would have to wait until nightfall, try to persuade the sailor on duty and see what would happen. We collected our things, evidently far too many for this particular plan. With great regret we farewelled all our friends and afterwards crossed through the main gates of the port and, burning our boats, set off on our maritime adventure.

POLIZONES
stowaways

We passed through customs without any difficulties and bravely headed toward our target. The chosen boat, the *San Antonio*, was at the center of the port's feverish activity. Because of its small size it didn't have to come right up alongside for the cranes to reach it and there was a gap of several meters between it and the docks. We had no choice but to wait until the boat moved closer before boarding, and so philosophically, we sat down on our bags to wait for the propitious moment. With the midnight change of shift the boat was brought alongside, but the harbormaster, a nasty character whose face disclosed his ill temper, stood squarely on the gangplank checking the arriving and departing workers. The crane driver, who in the meantime we had befriended, advised us to wait for a better moment because, he said, the master was a hostile bastard. So we began a long wait which lasted the whole night, warming ourselves in the crane, an ancient contraption that ran on steam. The sun rose to see us still waiting on the dock with our bags. Our hopes of boarding by stealth had almost completely dissipated when the captain turned up with a new, restored gangplank, and with it the *San Antonio* was now in permanent contact with dry land. Well-instructed by the crane driver, we slipped on board easily, making ourselves at home, and locked ourselves and our bags in the bathroom in the officers' quarters. From then on, all we had to do was say in a nasal little voice "excuse me, can't come in" or "it's occupied," on the half dozen or so times someone tried to open the door.

Twelve p.m. came fast and the boat sailed, but our joy was fast disappearing because the toilet, apparently blocked for some time, gave off an insufferable smell and the heat was intense. By 1 p.m., Alberto had vomited up everything that had been in his stomach, and by 5 p.m., dying of hunger and with the coast long out of sight, we presented ourselves to the captain as stowaways. He was surprised to see us again and in these particular circumstances, but to conceal his surprise in front of the other officers, he winked at us flamboyantly while asking in a thundering voice: "Do you two seriously believe that to go traveling the only thing you have to do is hide away in the first boat you find? Have you not thought through the consequences of doing exactly that?"

The truth is we hadn't thought through a thing.

He called the steward and charged him to give us work and something to eat. We devoured our rations contentedly, but when I learned that I would have to clean the famous toilet, the food caught in my throat. As I went below, swearing behind closed lips and followed by Alberto's amused glance, who was assigned to peel potatoes, I confess I felt tempted to forget everything ever written about the rules of friendship and request a change of jobs. There is no justice! He adds a good portion to the accumulated filth and I clean it up!

After conscientiously completing our work, the captain summoned us again. He recommended that we say nothing about our previous meeting and that he would ensure nothing happened when we arrived in Antofagasta, the ship's destination. He let us sleep in the cabin of an officer on leave, and that night invited us to play canasta and have a drink or two. After a rejuvenating sleep we got up, participating with full consent in the phrase, "New brooms sweep cleanly." We set to work with great diligence, determined to earn the price of our passage, with interest. By midday, however, we felt we were overdoing it and by the afternoon we became firmly convinced we were the purest pair of bums around. We thought we should get a good sleep, ready for work the next day, not to mention washing our dirty clothes, but the captain again invited us to play cards and that killed our good intentions.

It took the steward, sufficiently unfriendly, approximately one hour to get us up to begin working. My job was to clean the decks with kerosene, a task I worked at all day and still didn't finish. Alberto's string-pulling found him back in the kitchen, eating better food and more of it, not being too discriminating about what he was pouring into his stomach.

At night, after the exhausting games of canasta, we would look out over the immense sea, full of white-flecked and green reflections, the two of us leaning side by side on the railing, each of us far away, flying in his own aircraft to the stratospheric regions of his own dreams. There we understood that our vocation, our true vocation, was to move for eternity along the roads and seas of the world. Always curious, looking into everything that came before our eyes, sniffing out each corner but only ever faintly — not setting down roots in any land or staying long enough to see the substratum of things; the outer limits would suffice. As all the sentimental themes the sea inspires passed through our conversation, the lights of Antofagasta began to shine in the distance, to the northeast. It was the end of our adventure as stowaways, or at least the end of this adventure now that our boat was returning to Valparaíso.

ESTA VEZ, FRACASO
this time, disaster

I can see him now, clearly, the drunk captain, like all his officers and the owner of the vessel alongside with his great big mustache, their crude gestures the results of bad wine. And the wild laughter as they recounted our odyssey. "Hey listen, they're tigers, they're on your boat now for sure, you'll find out when you're out to sea." The captain must have let slip to his friend and colleague this or some similar phrase.

We didn't, of course, know any of this; an hour before sailing we were comfortably installed, totally buried in tons of perfumed melons, stuffing ourselves silly. We were talking about the sailors, who were the best, since with the complicity of one of them we had been able to get on board and hide ourselves away in such a very secure spot. And then we heard an irate voice, and a seemingly enormous mustache emerged from who knows where and plunged us into an appalling confusion. A long line of melon skins, perfectly peeled, was floating away Indian file on the tranquil sea. The rest was ignominious. The sailor told us afterwards, "I'd have got him off the scent, boys, but he saw the melons and it seems he went into a "batten down the hatches, don't let anyone escape" routine. And well," (he was fairly embarrassed) "you shouldn't have eaten so many melons!"

One of our traveling companions from the *San Antonio* summed up his brilliant life philosophy with one fine phrase: "Stop arsing about you assholes. Why don't you get off your asses and go back to your asshole country." So that's more or less what we did; we picked up our bags and set off for Chuquicamata, the famous copper mine.

But not straight away. There was a pause of one day while we waited for permission from the mine's authorities to visit and meanwhile we received an appropriate send-off from the enthusiastic Bacchanalian sailors.

Lying beneath the meager shade of two lampposts on the arid road leading to the mines, we spent a good part of the day yelling things at each other now and again from one post to another, until on the horizon appeared the asthmatic outline of the little truck which took us halfway, to a town called Baquedano.

There we made friends with a married couple, Chilean workers who were communists.* By the light of the single candle illuminating us, drinking *mate* and eating a piece of bread and cheese, the man's shrunken figure carried a mysterious, tragic air. In his simple and expressive language he recounted his three months in prison, and told us about his starving wife who stood by him with exemplary loyalty, his children — left in the care of a kindly neighbor, his fruitless pilgrimage in search of work and his *compañeros*, mysteriously disappeared and said to be somewhere at the bottom of the sea.

The couple, numb with cold, huddling against each other in the desert night, were a living representation of the proletariat in any part of the world. They had not one single miserable blanket to

*The Chilean Communist Party was banned and many members persecuted under the so-called Law for the Defense of Democracy (1948–58).

cover themselves with, so we gave them one of ours and Alberto and I wrapped the other around us as best we could. It was one of the coldest times in my life, but also one which made me feel a little more brotherly toward this strange, for me anyway, human species.

At eight the next morning we found a truck to take us to the town of Chuquicamata. We separated from the couple who were heading for the sulphur mines in the mountains where the climate is so bad and the living conditions so hard that you don't need a work permit and nobody asks you what your politics are. The only thing that matters is the enthusiasm with which the worker sets to ruining his health in search of a few meager crumbs that barely provide his subsistence.

Although the blurred silhouette of the couple was nearly lost in the distance separating us, we could still see the man's singularly determined face and we remembered his straightforward invitation: "Come, comrades, let's eat together. I, too, am a tramp," which showed his underlying disdain for the parasitic nature he saw in our aimless traveling.

It's a great pity that they repress people like this. Apart from whether collectivism, the "communist vermin," is a danger to decent life, the communism gnawing at his entrails was no more than a natural longing for something better, a protest against persistent hunger transformed into a love for this strange doctrine, whose essence he could never grasp but whose translation, "bread for the poor," was something he understood and, more importantly, that filled him with hope.

There, the bosses, the blond, efficient and arrogant managers, told us in primitive Spanish: "This isn't a tourist town. I'll find a guide to give you a half-hour tour around the mine's installations and then do us a favor and leave us alone, we have a lot of work to do." A strike was imminent. Yet the guide, faithful dog of the Yankee bosses, told us: "Imbecilic gringos, losing thousands of *pesos* every day in a strike so as not to give a poor worker a few more *centavos*. When my General Ibañez comes to power that'll all be over."* And a foreman-poet: "These are the famous grades that enable every inch of copper to be mined. Many people like you ask me technical questions but it is rare they ask how many lives it has cost. I can't answer you, doctors, but thank you for asking."

Cold efficiency and impotent resentment go hand in hand in the big mine, linked in spite of the hatred by the common necessity to live, on the one hand, and to speculate on the other... we will see whether one day, some miner will take up his pick in pleasure and go and poison his lungs with a conscious joy. They say that's what it's like over there, where the red blaze that now lights up the world comes from. So they say. I don't know.

CHUQUICAMATA
chuquicamata

Chuquicamata is like a scene from a modern drama. You cannot say that it's lacking in beauty, but it is a beauty without grace, imposing and glacial. As you come close to any part of the mine, the whole landscape seems to concentrate, giving a feeling of suffocation across the plain. There is a moment when, after 200 kilometers, the lightly shaded green of the little town of Calama interrupts

*Carlos Ibañez del Campo was Chilean President from 1952 to 1958. He was a populist, who promised to legalize the Communist Party if elected.

the monotonous gray and is greeted with joy, which as an authentic oasis in the desert it richly deserves. And what a desert! The weather observatory at Moctezuma, near "Chuqui," describes it as the driest in the world. The mountains, where not a single blade of grass can grow in the nitrate soil, are defenseless against attacks of wind and water. They display their gray spine, prematurely aged in the battle with the elements, their wrinkles that do not correspond to their real geological age. And how many of those mountains surrounding their famous brother enclose in their heavy wombs similar riches, as they wait for the soulless arms of the mechanical shovels to devour their insides, spiced as they would be with the inevitable human lives — the lives of the poor, unsung heroes of this battle, who die miserably in one of the thousand traps set by nature to defend its treasures, when all they want is to earn their daily bread.

Chuquicamata is essentially a great copper mountain with 20-meter-high terraces cut into its enormous sides, from where the extracted mineral is easily transported by rail. The unique formation of the vein means that extraction is entirely open cut, allowing large-scale exploitation of the ore-body, which grades one percent copper per ton of ore. Every morning the mountain is dynamited and huge mechanical shovels load the material on to rail wagons that take it to the grinder to be crushed. This crushing occurs over three consecutive passes, turning the raw material into a medium-fine gravel. It is then put in a sulphuric acid solution which extracts the copper in the form of sulphate, also forming a copper chloride, turning into ferrous chloride when it comes into contact with old iron. From there the liquid is taken to the so-called "green house" where the copper sulphate solution is put into huge baths and for a week submitted to a current of 30 volts, bringing about the electrolysis of the salt: the copper sticks to the thin sheets of the same metal, which have previously been formed in other baths with stronger solutions. After five or six days, the sheets are ready for the smelter; the solution has lost eight to 10 grams of sulphate per liter and is enriched with new quantities of the ground material. The sheets are then placed in furnaces that, after 12 hours smelting at 2,000 degrees centigrade, produce 350-pound ingots. Every night 45 wagons in convoy take over 20 tons of copper each down to Antofagasta, the result of a day's work.

This is a crude summary of the manufacturing process, which employs a floating population of 3,000 souls in Chuquicamata; but this process only extracts oxide ore. The Chile Exploration Company is building another plant to exploit the sulphate ore. This plant, the biggest of its kind in the world, has two 96-meter-high chimneys and will take over almost all future production, while the old plant will be slowly phased out since the oxide ore is about to run out. There is already an enormous stockpile of raw material to feed the new smelter and it will begin to be processed in 1954 when the plant is opened.

Chile produces 20 percent of the world's copper, and in these uncertain times of potential conflict copper has become vitally important because it is an essential component of various types of weapons of destruction. Hence, an economic and political battle is being waged in Chile between a coalition of nationalist and left-wing groupings that advocate nationalizing the mines, and those who, in the cause of free enterprise, prefer a well-run mine (even in foreign hands) to possibly less efficient management by the state. Serious accusations have been made in Congress against the companies currently exploiting the concessions, symptomatic of the climate of nationalist aspiration surrounding copper production.

Whatever the outcome of the battle, it would do well not to forget the lesson taught by the graveyards of the mines, containing only a small share of the immense number of people devoured by cave-ins, the silica and the hellish climate of the mountain.

KILOMETRAJE ÁRIDO
arid land for miles and miles

Now that we'd lost our water bottle, the problem of crossing the desert by foot became even worse. Still, without any apprehension we set off, leaving behind the barrier marking the limits of the town of Chuquicamata. Our pace was incredibly athletic while within sight of the town's inhabitants, but later the vast solitude of the bare Andes, the sun that fell harshly across our necks and the badly distributed weight of our backpacks brought us back to reality. Until what point our actions were "heroic," as one policeman put it, we're not sure, but we began to suspect, I think with good reason, that the definitive adjective was approximating something more like "stupid."

After two hours' walking, 10 kilometers at the most, we planted ourselves down in the shade of a sign saying I've no idea what, the only thing capable of offering us the slightest shelter from the rays of the sun. And there we stayed all day, shifting around to get the post's shade in our eyes at least.

We rapidly consumed the liter of water we had brought with us and by late afternoon, with gargantuan thirsts, we set off back towards the sentry post at the town's limits, totally defeated.

We spent the night there, seeking refuge inside the little room, where a bright fire maintained the pleasant temperature despite the cold outside. The nightwatchman, with proverbial Chilean hospitality, shared his food with us, a pathetic feast after a whole day of fasting, but better than nothing.

At dawn the next day the truck of a cigarette company passed and took us closer to our destination; but while continuing directly on to the port of Tocopilla, we were thinking of heading north to

Ilave, so it dropped us where the roads crossed. We started walking enthusiastically towards a house we knew was eight kilometers up the road, but only halfway there we became tired and resolved to have a little nap. We hung one of our blankets between a telegraph post and a distance marker and got under it — a Turkish bath for our bodies and a sunbath for our feet.

Two or three hours later, when we'd lost about three liters of water each, a small Ford passed by containing three noble citizens, all roaring drunk and singing *cuecas** at full blast. They were striking workers from the mine called Magdalena, celebrating the victory of the people's cause a little prematurely by getting happily plastered. The drunks took us as far as a local railroad station. There we encountered a group of laborers practising for a football match with a rival team. Alberto took a pair of running shoes out of his backpack and started to sound off. The result was spectacular. We were signed up for the match on the following Sunday; in return: food, board and transport to Iquique.

Two days until Sunday arrived, marked by a splendid victory for our team and a barbecue of goats prepared by Alberto, astounding the assembled gathering with the art of Argentine cooking. Those two days we dedicated to visiting some of the many nitrate-purifying plants in that area of Chile.

It really isn't very difficult for mining companies to extract the mineral wealth of this part of the world. There's nothing more to do besides scraping off the top layer containing the mineral and transporting it to huge baths where it's submitted to a fairly uncomplicated separating process to extract the nitrates, saltpeter and mud. Apparently the Germans had the first concessions but their plants were expropriated and they are now largely British owned. Workers at the two biggest mines in terms of both production and workforce were at the time on strike and the mines were south of where we were heading, so we decided not to visit them. We went

*Chilean folk dances.

instead to quite a big plant, La Victoria, which has at its entrance a plaque marking the place where Hector Supicci Sedes died, the brilliant Uruguayan rally driver who was hit by another driver as he came out of a refuelling pit stop.

A succession of trucks took us all over the region until we finally reached Iquique warmly wrapped in blankets of alfalfa, cargo of the truck that took us the last leg. Our arrival, with the sun rising behind us, casting our reflections against the purest blue of the morning sea, seemed like something out of *A Thousand and One Nights.* As if it were a magic carpet the truck appeared, fluttering on the cliff faces above the port, and as first gear slowed our winding and groaning flight downward we saw from our vantage point the whole city rising to meet us.

In Iquique there wasn't a single boat, Argentine or any other kind, so it was useless staying in the port and we decided to scrounge a lift on the first truck leaving for Arica.

ACABA CHILE
the end of chile

The long kilometers stretching between Iquique and Arica climb and descend the whole way. We were carried from arid tablelands to valleys with only slight trickles of water running through them, barely sufficient for a few small, stunted trees to grow at their edges. These utterly desolate pampas emit a sultry heat during the day, though as with all desert climates it is considerably cooler by night. The thought that Valdivia came through this way with his handful of men, traveling 50 or 60 kilometers a day without discovering a drop of water or even some shrub to shelter from the hottest hours, leaves a strong impression. Knowledge of the terrain actually crossed by the *conquistadores* automatically elevates Valdivia's feat to one of the most notable of Spanish colonization, without doubt superior to the those that endure in the history of America because more fortunate explorers found wealthy kingdoms at the end of their adventurous wars, turning the sweat of their conquest into gold.

Valdivia's actions symbolize man's indefatigable thirst to take control of a place where he can exercise total authority. That phrase, attributed to Caesar, proclaiming he would rather be first-in-command in some humble Alpine village than second-in-command in Rome, is repeated less pompously, but no less effectively, in the epic campaign that is the conquest of Chile. If, in the moment the *conquistador* was facing death at the hands of that invincible Araucanian Caupolicán, he had not been overwhelmed like a hunted animal, with fury, I do not doubt that judging his life, Valdivia would have felt his death was fully justified. He belonged to that special class of men the species produces every so often, in whom a craving for limitless power is so extreme that any suffering to achieve it seems natural, and he had become the omnipotent ruler of a warrior nation.

Arica is a sweet little port which hasn't yet lost the memory of its previous owners, the Peruvians, and it forms a kind of meeting point between the two countries, so different in spite of their geographical proximity and common ancestry. The promontory, pride of the town, rises 100 meters in an imposing mass of sheer rock face. The palm trees, the heat, the subtropical fruit sold in the markets, lend it the unique physiognomy of a Caribbean town, or something like that, completely different from its colleagues further south.

A doctor, who showed us as much disrespect as an established, financially secure bourgeois can show to a couple of hobos (even hobos with titles), permitted us to sleep in the town's hospital. Early the next day we fled the unwelcoming place, heading straight for the border with Peru. But first we bade farewell to the Pacific with one last swim (soap and everything) and it served to awaken a dormant yearning in Alberto: to eat seafood. We began a patient search for clams and other seafood on the beach by some cliffs. We ate something salty and slimy, but it didn't distract us from our hunger or satisfy Alberto's craving, in fact it wouldn't even have made a prisoner happy. The slime was repulsive and, with nothing on it, worse.

We set off at our usual time, after eating at the police station, marking out our track along the coast until the border. A van, however, picked us up and we reached the border post installed in comfort. We met a customs officer who had worked on the Argentine border, and acknowledging and appreciating our passion for *mate* he gave us hot water, cookies and, best of all, found us a ride to Tacna. The police chief welcomed us amiably at the border with a several pretentious inanities about Argentines in Peru and with a handshake, we said goodbye to that hospitable Chilean land.

CHILE, OJEADA DE LEJOS
chile, a vision from afar

When I made these travel notes, hot and fresh with enthusiasm, I wrote some things that were perhaps a little flashy and somewhat removed from the intended spirit of scientific inquiry. And it's probably not appropriate now, more than a year after writing them, to give my current opinions about Chile; I'd prefer to review what I wrote then.

Ernesto Guevara and La Poderosa II, 1951.

"Suddenly, slipping in as if part of our fantasy,
the question arose:
'Why don't we go to North America?'
'North America, but how?'
'On La Poderosa, man'."

Ernesto Guevara and Alberto Granado.

"My most important mission before leaving was to take exams in as many subjects as possible; Alberto's to prepare the bike for the long journey and to study and plan our route."

Self-Portrait, by Ernesto Guevara, in Argentina, 1951.

Ernesto Guevara and a friend in Buenos Aires,
Argentina, 1951.

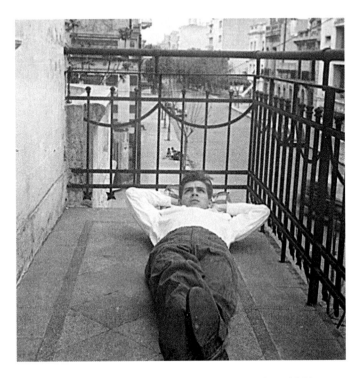

Ernesto Guevara in Buenos Aires, Argentina, 1951.

Alberto Granado (front left), Ernesto Guevara (center with cap) and friends, with La Poderosa II, 1951, when Ernesto and Alberto had just begun their adventure.

Alberto Granado attempting to scale the Argentine Andes, near San Martín de los Andes. Photograph by Ernesto Guevara, January 1952.

"After some minutes of joking about in the patch of snow crowning the peak, we took to the task of descending... Alberto lost his goggles and my pants were reduced to rags."

Alberto Granado on board the *Modesta Victoria*, crossing into
Chile. Photograph taken by Ernesto Guevara from Lago
Nahuel Huapí, February 1952.

"A gentle sun illuminated the new day, our day of departure,
our farewell to Argentine soil. Carrying the bike on to the
Modesta Victoria was not an easy task, but with patience
we eventually did it."

Alberto Granado (center) with two friends from Córdoba, climbing Santa Lucía in Santiago de Chile. Photograph taken by Ernesto Guevara, March 1952.

"The following day we climbed up Santa Lucía, a rocky formation in the center of the city with its own particular history, and were peacefully performing the task of photographing the city when a convoy of Suquía members arrived..."

On the road from Taratá to Puno, Peru. (Ernesto third from left). Photograph taken by Alberto Granado, March 25, 1952.

"The spectacle offered by the two of us drinking our strange brew (*mate*) must have seemed as interesting to the Indians as their traditional dress seemed to us, because not a moment passed without one of them approaching to ask in broken Spanish just why we were pouring water into that rare artefact."

The view of Cuzco from the fortress Sascahuáman.
Photograph taken by Alberto or Ernesto, April 1952.

"High above the city another Cuzco can be seen, displacing
the destroyed fortress: a Cuzco with colored-tile roofs... and as
the city falls away it shows us only its narrow streets and its
native inhabitants dressed in typical costume,
all the local colors."

Detail of the Church of Santo Domingo, erected over the ruins of the Temple of the Sun. Photograph by Alberto or Ernesto, April 1952.

"The temples to Inti were razed to their foundations or their walls were made to serve the ascent of the churches of the new religion: the cathedral was erected over the remains of a grand palace, and above the walls of the Temple of the Sun rose the Church of Santo Domingo, lesson and punishment from the proud conqueror."

Pisac, a village in the Peruvian Andes. Photograph taken by
Alberto or Ernesto, April 1952.

"After trekking for two long hours along a rough path we
reached the peak of Pisac; arriving there as well, though long
before us, were the swords of the Spanish soldiers, destroying
Pisac's defenders, defenses and even its temple."

The fortress of Ollantaytambo. Photographs taken by
Ernesto Guevara, April 1952.

"Tracing the course of the Vilcanota and passing by some
relatively unimportant sites, we reached Ollantaytambo, a vast
fortress where [the Inca] Manco II rose up in arms against the
Spanish, resisting Hernando Pizarro's troops and founding the
minor dynasty of the Four Incas."

Macchu Pichu and Huayna Pichu. Photograph taken by
Alberto or Ernesto, April 5, 1952.

"The most important and irrefutable thing, however, is that
here we found the pure expression of the most powerful
indigenous race in the Americas – still clean of contact with a
conquering civilization and replete with immensely evocative
treasures... The spectacular landscape circling the fortress
supplies an essential backdrop, inspiring dreamers to wander
its ruins for the sake of it."

The María Angola Cathedral. Photograph taken by Ernesto or Alberto, April 1952.

"The cost of restoring the cathedral bell towers, destroyed by the earthquake in 1950, had been met by General Franco's [Spanish] government, and as a gesture of gratitude the band was ordered to play the Spanish national anthem...
I couldn't say whether with good intentions or bad, the band had [instead] struck up the Spanish republican anthem."

The Cathedral of Cuzco. Photograph taken by
Ernesto or Alberto, April 1952.

"The glitz of the brilliant interior reflects a glorious past...
Gold doesn't have the gentle dignity of silver which becomes
more charming as it ages, and so the cathedral seems to be
decorated like an old woman with too much makeup. There is
real artistry in the choir stalls, made from wood by Indian or
mestizo craftsmen. In their carved scenes of the lives of the
saints, they have infused the cedar with the spirit of the
Catholic Church and the enigmatic soul of the
true Andean peoples."

Alberto Granado (second from left) with the Cambalache
brothers in Pucallpa, Peru. Photograph taken by
Ernesto Guevara, May 1952.

"We left in a hurry the next morning, before the woman who
owned the place woke up, because we hadn't paid the bill and
the Camba brothers were short on cash because of
repairs to the axle."

Alberto Granado fishing with staff from the San Pablo leper
colony. Photograph taken by Ernesto Guevara,
June 1952.

"Thursday is a day of rest for the colony so we changed our
routine, not visiting the compound. We tried to fish, without
success, in the morning. In the afternoon we played football
and my performance in goal was less atrocious."

A tribe of Yagua Indians with Alberto Granado (holding child) and Dr. Bresciani (left), the director of the San Pablo leper colony. Photograph taken by Ernesto Guevara, June 1952.

"Sunday in the morning we visited a tribe of Yaguas, the Indians of the red straw... Their way of living was fascinating – outside, beneath wooden planks and with tiny, hermetic palm frond huts to shelter in at night from the mosquitoes that attack in close formation."

An Indian man with Alberto Granado (left) and Dr. Bresciani.
Photograph taken by Ernesto Guevara, June 1952.

"The kids have distended bellies and are rather scrawny but
the older people show no signs of vitamin deficiency, in
contrast with its rate among more developed people living in
the jungle. Their diet consists of yucca, bananas and palm
fruit, mixed with the animals they hunt with rifles."

Ernesto Guevara and Alberto Granado aboard the
Mambo-Tango, June 1952.

"The raft was almost ready, only needing oars. That night an
assembly of the colony's patients gave us a farewell serenade,
with lots of local songs sung by a blind man. The orchestra was
made up of a flute player, a guitarist and an accordion player
with almost no fingers, and a 'healthy' contingent helping out
with a saxophone, a guitar and some percussion."

Ernesto Guevara and Alberto Granado aboard the
Mambo-Tango, sailing down the Amazon River, June 1952.

"We rowed at full strength and just when it seemed we were
definitely on our way, we'd turn a half circle and head back
into mid-stream. We watched with growing desperation as the
lights drifted into the distance. Exhausted, we decided that at
least we could win the fight against the mosquitoes and sleep
peacefully until dawn."

Beginning with our expertise, medicine: the panorama of health care in Chile leaves a lot to be desired (although I realized later it was by far superior to that in other countries I got to know). Free, public hospitals are extremely rare and even in those posters announcing the following appear: "Why do you complain about your treatment if you are not contributing to the maintenance of this hospital?" Generally speaking, medical attention in the north is free, but hospital accommodation has to be paid for, and prices range from petty sums to virtual monuments to legalized theft. Sick or injured workers at the Chuquicamata mine receive medical attention and hospital treatment for five Chilean *escudos* a day, but someone not working at the mine would pay between 300 and 500 *escudos* a day. Hospitals have no money and they lack medicine and adequate facilities. We have seen filthy operating rooms with pitiful lighting, and not just in small towns but even in Valparaíso. There aren't enough surgical instruments. The bathrooms are dirty. Awareness of hygiene is poor. It's a Chilean custom (afterwards I saw it across practically all of South America) not to throw used toilet paper in the toilet but on to the floor or in the boxes provided.

The standard of living in Chile is lower than in Argentina. On top of the very low wages paid in the south, unemployment is high and the authorities afford workers very little protection (although it's better than is provided in the north of the continent). Veritable waves of Chileans are driven by all this into emigrating to Argentina, in search of the legendary city of gold which cunning political propaganda has offered those who live to the west of the Andes. In the north, workers in the copper, nitrate, gold and sulphur mines are better paid, but life is much more expensive, and they lack in general many essential consumer items and the mountain climate is cruel. It brings to mind the meaningful shrug with which a manager at Chuquicamata answered my questions regarding compensation paid to the families of the 10,000 or more workers interred in the local cemetery.

The political scene is confusing (this was written before the elections in which Ibañez triumphed). There are four presidential candidates, of whom Carlos Ibáñez del Campo seems most likely to win. A retired soldier with dictatorial tendencies and political ambitions similar to those of Perón, he inspires his people with all the enthusiasm of a caudillo. His base of power is the Popular Socialist Party, behind which various minor factions are united. Second in line, as far as I can see, is Pedro Enrique Alfonso, the official government candidate, who is politically ambiguous; he seems to be friendly with the Americans and courts almost all the other parties. The champion of the right is the tycoon Arturo Matte Larraín, the son-in-law of the late President Alessandri who counts the support of all the reactionary sectors of the population. Last on the list is the Popular Front candidate Salvador Allende,* who is supported by the communists even though they have seen their voting power reduced by 40,000, the number of people denied the right to vote because of their affiliation to the Communist Party.

It's likely that Ibañez will observe a politics of Latin Americanism, manipulating hate for the United States to gain popularity; nationalizing the copper mines and others (although the fact that the United States owns huge Peruvian mineral deposits and is practically ready to begin exploiting them, doesn't greatly increase my confidence that nationalization of these Chilean mines will be feasible, at least in the short term); continue nationalizing the railroads and substantially enlarge Argentine-Chilean trade.

Chile as a country offers economic promise to any person disposed to work for it, so long as they don't belong to the proletariat: I mean, anyone who has a certain dose of education and technical knowledge. The land has the capacity to sustain enough livestock (especially sheep) and cereals to provide for its population. There are the necessary mineral resources to transform it into a powerful industrial country: iron, copper, coal, tin, gold, silver, manganese

*In 1970, Allende was elected as Chilean President. In 1973, a U.S.-backed coup installed General Augusto Pinochet's dictatorship, lasting 17 years.

and nitrates. The biggest effort Chile should make is to shake its uncomfortable Yankee friend from its back, a task that for the moment at least is Herculean, given the quantity of dollars the United States has invested here and the ease with which it flexes its economic muscle whenever its interests seem threatened.

TARATA, EL MUNDO NUEVO
tarata, the new world

Scarcely a few meters separated us from the Civil Guard post marking the limits of the town, but already our backpacks felt a hundred times heavier than they were. The sun stung us but as always we were wrapped in too many clothes for the hour of the day, though later we'd get very cold. The road climbed quickly and in no time we had passed the pyramid we'd seen from the village, built in homage to those Peruvians who died in the war with Chile.* We decided it would be a good place to make our first stop and test our luck with the passing trucks. All we could see in the direction of the road was a barren hillside, with barely any vegetation; placid Tacna, with its little dirt streets and terracotta roofs, waited so far in the distance it seemed almost daunting. The first truck to pass caused us great turmoil; we stuck our thumbs out apprehensively and to our surprise the driver stopped just ahead of us. Alberto took command of the operation, explaining in words that by now were very familiar to me, the purpose of our journey and asking him for

*Chile annexed the mineral-rich Atacarna desert in the so-called "Nitrate Wars" of 1879–83.

a lift; the driver gave an affirmative nod, indicating we should climb in the back, with a whole band of Indians.

Collecting our bags and crazy with gratitude, we were about to climb up when he called out to us: "Five *soles* to Tarata, you know that, right?" Alberto, furious, asked why he'd said nothing earlier, when we'd asked to be taken free of charge. The driver wasn't sure exactly what "free of charge" meant, but to Tarata it was five *soles*...

"And every one of them will be like that," Alberto said angrily, in that simple phrase directing all of his frustration toward me, who had suggested the idea in the first place of walking out of town to hitch a lift, rather than wait there like he wanted to do. The moment became decisive. We could go back, in which case we'd be admitting defeat, or we could continue on foot, letting whatever would happen, happen. We decided on the second course and started walking. It soon became apparent that our choice was not altogether wise: the sun was about to set and all around there was a total absence of life. Still, we supposed that so close to the village there would be some shack or other and, sustained by this illusion, we carried on.

It was soon pitch dark and we hadn't encountered a single sign of habitation. Even worse, we had no water with which to cook or brew *mate*. The cold intensified; the desert climate and the altitude we had reached turned the screw. Our exhaustion was unbelievable. We resolved simply to lay out our blankets over the ground and sleep until dawn. There was no moon, and the night was very dark, so we felt our way around spreading our blankets and wraped ourselves up as well as we could.

After five minutes Alberto informed me he was frozen solid; I responded that my poor body was even colder. But this wasn't a competition in refrigeration, so we decided to tackle the situation and search for some twigs to make a small fire and to occupy our hands. The result was unsurprisingly pathetic. Between us we managed a handful of sticks, making a timid fire incapable of heating anything at all. The hunger was grating but the cold much more so, to the point where we could no longer lie there just watching the four embers of our fire. We had to pack up camp and walk on in the dark. At first, to get warm, we set a fast pace and in no time we were desperate for breath. Under my jacket I felt the sweat running off me, but my feet were numb with cold and the sharp wind cut our faces like a knife. After two hours we were exhausted and my watch said only 12:30 a.m. A hopeful estimate gave us at least five hours of night to go. Further debate and another shot at sleeping between our blankets. After five minutes we were on our way again. The night was still young when we saw head lights in the distance; it wasn't something to get too excited about — the chances of getting a ride were bad — but at least the road was lit up. And that's how it went, the truck passed us by, indifferent in the face of our frantic shouts, and its lights exposed a deserted wasteland; no trees, no houses. Then confusion descended, every minute was slower than the one before until eventually the minutes became hours. Two or three times a distant dog's bark gave us some hope, but the pitch black night disclosed nothing and the dogs fell silent or moved off other directions.

At six in the morning we saw two huts by the edge of the road, illuminated in the clear, gray light of dawn. The last few meters we traveled in a flash, as if we had no weight at all on our backs. It seemed that we had never been welcomed with such friendliness, that we had never eaten bread and cheese like they sold us, or had such revitalizing *mate*. We were like demigods to these simple people: Alberto brandished his doctor's certificate for them, and moreover we had come from that wonderful country Argentina, where Perón lived with his wife Evita, where the poor have as much as the rich and the Indian isn't exploited or treated as severely as he is in this country. We answered thousands of questions about our country and its way of life. With the night chill still deeply embedded in our bones, our rose-colored imagery transformed Argentina into an alluring vision of the past. Our spirits lifted by the timid kindness of the *cholos*,* we made for a nearby dry riverbed, in which we spread our blankets and slept, caressed by the rising sun.

At 12 we set off again, much happier, the previous night's suffering forgotten, following old Vizcacha's advice.** The road was long though and we were soon pausing with notable frequency. We stopped for a rest at five in the afternoon, observing apathetically the approaching outline of a truck. As usual it was transporting a cargo of human livestock, the most profitable business of all there. But to our surprise, the truck stopped and we saw the Civil Guard from Tacna waving happily to us and inviting us to climb on; the invitation, of course, did not need to be repeated. The Aymara Indians in the back looked at us curiously but didn't dare to ask anything. Alberto tried to start a conversation with some of them, though their Spanish was bad. The truck continued to climb through an absolutely desolate landscape where only a few struggling thorn bushes gave any appearance of being alive. Then, suddenly, the grumbling with which the truck made its way higher gave way to a sigh of relief as we levelled out on to the plateau. We entered the town of Estaque and the view was incredible; our ecstatic eyes fixed themselves momentarily on the landscape extending around us and then we had to find out the names and explanations for all the things we saw. The Aymaras could barely understand us but the few indications they gave, in confused Spanish, only increased the emotional impact of the surroundings. We were in a legendary valley, whose evolution had been suspended several hundred years ago, and we happy 20th century mortals had today been given the good fortune to see. The irrigation channels — built by the Incas for the well-being of their subjects — flowed from the mountain into the valley, forming a thousand little waterfalls and running back and

---

*Indians or mestizos.
**A character from "Martín Fierro," an epic poem of gaucho life by the Argentine José Hernández.

forth across the road as it spiralled down. Ahead of us, low clouds hid the tops of the mountains, but in some of the clear spaces you could just make out snow falling on the highest peaks, little by little turning them white. The different crops cultivated by the Indians, carefully grown in terraced beds, allowed us to penetrate a new realm of botanical science: *oca, quinua, canihua, rocoto,* maize. We saw people wearing the same dress as the Indians in the truck, in their natural surroundings. They wore short, sadly colored woollen ponchos, tight calf-length pants, and sandals made from rope or old car tires. Absorbing everything we saw, we continued down the valley to Tarata. In Aymara this means the apex, or place of confluence, and it's been well-named since it stands within a great V formed by the mountain chains that are the town's guardians. It is an ancient, gentle village where life continues on a course it has traveled for centuries. The colonial church must be an archaeological gem because even more than its age it marks a union of imported European art with the spirit of the local Indians. In the narrow lanes of the town, its hugely uneven streets paved in local stone, the Indian women with their children on their backs... in short, in every typical scene, the town's very breath evokes the time before Spanish colonization. But the people before us are not the same proud race that repeatedly rose up against Inca rule, forcing them to maintain a permanent army on their borders; these people who watch us walk through the streets of the town are a defeated race. Their stares are tame, almost fearful, and completely indifferent to the outside world. Some give the impression they go on living only because it's a habit they cannot shake. The Civil Guard took us to the police station where they gave us board and some of the officers invited us to eat. We walked around town and then rested for a while since at three in the morning we were heading off to Puno on a passenger truck, which thanks to the Civil Guard was taking us for free.

EN LOS DOMINIOS DE LA PACHAMAMA
in the dominion of pachamama

The blankets of the Peruvian police had by three in the morning demonstrated their value, swathing us in restorative warmth. Then the policeman on guard shook us awake — there was a truck heading for Ilave — and we found ourselves in the sad situation of having to leave them behind. The night was magnificent, if terribly cold, and we were granted the privilege of some planks to sit on, separating us from the foul-smelling and flea-ridden human flock below us, their potent but warm stink like a virtual lasso. Only as the vehicle began its ascent did we realize the magnitude of the concession: nothing of the smell came close and it would have been difficult for a single, athletic flea to spring on to us for refuge. On the other hand the wind lashed liberally against our bodies and within minutes we were literally frozen. The truck continued to climb and with every minute the cold became more intense. To stop ourselves falling off we had to keep our hands free outside the more or less protective blankets; it was difficult to shift position even slightly without coming close to head first flight into the back of the truck. Close to dawn, some carburettor problem afflicting every engine at this altitude, caused the truck to stop; we were nearing the highest point of the road, almost 5,000 meters. In some corners of the sky the sun was rising and a vague light replaced the total darkness accompanying us until then. The psychological effects of the sun are strange: it had not yet appeared over the horizon and we already felt comforted, just imagining the heat it would bring.

On one side of the road huge semi-spherical fungi were growing — the only vegetation in the region — and we used it to make a pathetic fire, but it served to heat water from a little bit of snow.

The spectacle offered by the two of us drinking our strange brew must have seemed as interesting to the Indians as their traditional dress seemed to us, because not a moment passed without one of them approaching to ask in broken Spanish just why we were pouring water into that rare artefact. The truck categorically refused to take us any further, so all of us had to walk about three kilometers in the snow. It was remarkable to see the Indians treading through the snow, their bare calloused feet not seeming to worry them, while we felt our toes freeze in the intense cold, despite our boots and woolly socks. At a weary, steady pace, they trotted along like llamas in single file.

Saved from its awful episode, the truck continued with renewed passion and we soon cleared the highest pass, where there was a strange pyramid made of irregular-sized stones and crowned with a cross. As the truck passed, almost everyone spat and one or two crossed themselves. Intrigued, we asked what the significance of this strange ritual was but only the most complete of silences met us.

The sun was warming up and the temperature became more agreeable as we descended, always following the course of a river we had seen begin at the summit of the mountain and grow to a fair size. Snowcapped peaks looked down on us from all sides and herds of llamas and alpacas looked on without expression as the truck drove past, while several uncivilized vicuñas fled the disturbance.

At one of the many stops we made along the road an Indian timidly approached us, with his son who spoke good Spanish, and began to ask us all about the wonderful "land of Perón." Our imaginations ignited by the spectacular grandeur we were traveling through, it was easy for us to paint extraordinary events, embellishing to our hearts' desire the *capo's* exploits, filling the minds of our listeners with stories of the idyllic, beautiful life in our country. Through his son, the man asked us for a copy of the Argentine constitution with its declaration of the rights of the elderly, and we enthusiastically promised to send him one. When we resumed the trip, the old Indian took an appetizing corncob from beneath his clothes and offered it to us. We finished it off quickly, democratically dividing the kernels between us.

In the middle of the afternoon with the heavy, gray sky bearing down on us, we passed an interesting place where erosion had worn the huge boulders on the roadside into feudalistic castles. They had battlements, gargoyles observing us disconcertingly, and a host of fabulous monsters that seemed to be standing guard, minding the tranquillity for the mythical characters who surely inhabited the place. The slight drizzle, which for some time had brushed our faces, became stronger and turned into a heavy downpour. The driver called out to the "Argentine doctors," inviting us into his cabin, the height of comfort in those parts. We immediately made friends with a schoolteacher from Puno, whom the government had sacked for being a member of the APRA party [American Popular Revolutionary Alliance]. The man, who clearly had indigenous blood and who moreover was an "Aprista" — which meant nothing to us — had many incredible stories of Indian custom and culture, delighting us with a thousand anecdotes and memories of his life as a teacher. Following the call of his Indian blood, he had sided with the Aymaras in the never-ending debates among the experts on the region, against the Coyas whom he qualified as cowardly *ladinos*.*

He also gave us the key to the strange ritual observed by our traveling companions earlier in the day. Arriving at the highest point of the mountain the Indian gifts all of his sadness to Pachamama, Mother Earth, in the symbolic form of a stone, which gradually amass to shape the pyramids we had seen. When the Spaniards arrived to conquer the region they tried immediately to destroy such

*Spanish-speaking Latin Americans, often used to refer to Indians who adopt Spanish ways.

beliefs and abolish such rituals, but without success. So the Spanish monks decided to accept the inevitable, placing a single cross atop each pile of stones. All this took place four centuries ago (as told by Garcilaso de la Vega*) and judging by the number of Indians who made the sign of the cross, the religious didn't make a lot of progress. The rise of modern transport has meant the faithful now spit out chewed coca-leaves instead of placing stones, and this carries their troubles to rest with Pachamama.

The inspired voice of the teacher rose to a resounding pitch whenever he spoke about his Indians, the once rebellious Aymara race who had held the Inca armies in check, and it fell to a vacant depth when he spoke of the Indians' present condition, brutalized by modern civilization and by their *compañeros*, his bitter enemies the mestizos, who heap revenge on the Aymaras for their own position halfway between two worlds. He spoke of the need to build schools that would orient individuals within their own world, enable them to play a useful role within it; of the need to change fundamentally the present system of education, which, on the rare occasion it does offer Indians education (according only to white man's criteria) simply fills them with shame and resentment, rendering them unable to help their fellow Indians and at the severe disadvantage of having to fight within a hostile white society which refuses to accept them. The destiny of those unhappy individuals is to stagnate in some minor bureaucratic position and to die hoping that one of their children, thanks to the miracle powers of a drop of colonizing blood in their veins, might somehow achieve the goal they look forward to until their last days. In the convulsive clenching of his fist one could perceive the confession of a man tormented by his own misfortune and also the very desire he attributed to his hypothetical example. Wasn't he in fact a typical product of an "education" which damages the person receiving its favor, a con-

*The Inca Garcilaso, son of an Inca princess and a *conquistador*, was one of the chroniclers of the conquest.

cession to the magic power of that single "drop," even if it came from some poor mestizo woman sold to a local *cacique** or was the result of an Indian maid's rape by her drunken Spanish master?

But our journey was almost over and the teacher fell silent. The road curved and we crossed a bridge over the same river we had first seen early that morning as a tiny stream. Ilave was on the other side.

EL LAGO DEL SOL
lake of the sun

The sacred lake revealed only a small part of its grandeur. The narrow tongue of land surrounding the bay Puno is built on, hid it from view. Reed canoes bobbed here and there in the tranquil water and a few fishing boats filed out through the lake's entrance. The wind was very cold and the smothering, leaden sky seemed to replicate our state of mind. Although we had come directly to Puno, without stopping in llave and had secured temporary lodging and a good meal at the local barracks, our luck seemed to have run out. Very politely the commanding officer had shown us the door, explaining that as this was a border checkpoint foreign civilians were strictly forbidden from staying overnight.

We didn't want to go without exploring the lake, so we went to the pier to see if anyone would take us out in a boat, where we

*A local political boss.

could admire the lake in all its magnitude. We used an interpreter to advance the operation because none of the fishermen, all pure Aymara, knew any Spanish at all. For a modest sum of five *soles*, we managed to get them to take both of us and the intrusive guide who was sticking to us. We considered swimming in the lake, but after testing the temperature with the tips of our little fingers we thought better of it (Alberto made a big show of taking off his clothes and boots, only to put them back on again, of course).

Like tiny pinpoints dispersed across the vast, gray surface of the lake, a group of islands emerged in the distance. Our interpreter described the lives of the fishermen there, some of whom have barely ever seen a white man, and who live according to the old ways, eating the same food, fishing with 500-year-old techniques and keeping their costumes, rituals and traditions alive.

When we returned to the port, we walked over to one of the boats running between Puno and a Bolivian port to try and get some *mate*, which we were low on. But they drink almost no *mate* in the north of Bolivia, in fact they'd hardly heard of it, and we couldn't even get a half-kilo. We examined the boat which had been designed in England and built here; its lavishness clashed with the general poverty of the whole region.

Our problem of lodging found its solution at the Civil Guard post, where a very friendly lieutenant let us stay in the infirmary, the two of us in one bed but at least we were cosy and warm. After a pretty interesting visit to the cathedral the following day, we found a truck heading for Cuzco. The doctor in Puno had given us letter of introduction for Dr. Hermosa — and ex-leprologist now living in Cuzco.

The first leg of the journey wasn't too long as the truck driver left us in Juliaca, from where we had to find another truck to take us (ever northward). We went, of course, on the recommendation of Puno's Civil Guard, to the police station where we found a very drunk sergeant. He took a liking to us and invited us for a drink, ordering beers that were downed in one, all except for mine which remained full on the table.

"What's the matter, my Argentine friend, don't you drink?"

"No, it's not that; in my country we don't normally drink like this. Don't feel bad, it's just that we only drink if we're eating at the same time."

"But, *cheee,*" he said, his nasal voice accentuating our country's onomatopoeic nickname, "Why didn't you say so?" With a clap of his hands he ordered some great cheese sandwiches — and I was fairly satisfied with that. Then he swept himself away into euphoric descriptions of his various heroic deeds, boasting about the fear and respect held for him by the people of the region because of his fabulous marksmanship. To prove it he pulled out his gun and said to Alberto: "Look, *cheee,* stand 20 meters away with a cigarette in your mouth and if I can't light it with the first bullet, I'll give you 50 *soles.*" Alberto doesn't like money that much and he wasn't about to move from his chair, at least not for 50 *soles.* "Come on *cheee,* I'll make it 100." Alberto didn't move a muscle.

When he got to 200 *soles* — laid out on the table — Alberto's eyes began to flicker, but his instinct for self-preservation was stronger and he still didn't move. So the sergeant took off his cap and, watching through a mirror, tossed it behind him and fired. The cap was still in perfect condition, of course, but the wall wasn't and the owner of the bar flew into a fury, storming off to the police station to complain.

Within minutes an officer showed up to find out what the scandal was all about, hauling the sergeant into a corner to give him a talking to. When they rejoined our group the sergeant launched into a tirade against my traveling buddy, also making faces at him so he'd get the point: "Listen up, Argentine, got any more firecrackers like that one you just let off?" Alberto caught on quickly and said, his face the picture of innocence, that he had run out. The officer gave him a warning about letting off fireworks in public places, then told the owner that the incident was over; he could see no sign on the wall that any gun had been fired. The woman went to ask the sergeant to shift a few centimeters from where he was located, standing rigidly against the wall, but a quick mental calculation of the pros and cons was enough for her to keep her mouth shut on that score and instead give Alberto an extra tongue lashing. "These Argentines think they own everything," she said, plus a few more insults that were lost in the distance as we fled, one of us thinking wistfully of the beer, the other of the lost sandwiches.

We found another truck to ride in, traveling with a couple of young guys from Lima. The whole time they tried to show us how much better they were than the silent Indians, who endured their taunts and showed no sign of being bothered. At first we looked the other way, paying them no attention, but after some hours the tedious journey across an interminable plain forced us to exchange a few words with the only other white people on board, the only ones we could chat with since the wary Indians barely dignified our questions, offering only monosyllabic replies. In truth these boys from Lima were normal enough, they just needed to make the differences between them and the Indians clear. As we chewed vigorously on the coca leaves our newfound friends had diligently obtained for us, a flood of tangos engulfed our unsuspecting companions.

We arrived at last light in a village called Ayaviry, where we stayed in a hotel paid for by the head of the Civil Guard. "Excuse me," he responded, to our feeble protest against his startling gesture. "Two Argentine doctors sleeping rough because they have no money? It can't be." But in spite of the warm bed, we could barely keep our eyes closed: throughout the night, the coca we'd ingested revenged our bravado in floods of nausea, colic and severe headache.

We left very early the next morning in the same truck, for Sicuani where we arrived in the middle of the afternoon overwhelmed by too much cold, rain and hunger. As always we spent the night at the Civil Guard post and as always they looked after us well. A miserable little river called the Vilcanota runs through Sicuani, and we would be following the course of its water, an ocean of mud, for a while.

In the Sicuani market we were pondering the whole range of colors overflowing from the stalls, tangling with the vendors' monotonous cries and the monotone buzz of the crowd, when we noticed a gathering of people on a corner and went to investigate.

Surrounded by a dense, silent multitude a procession advanced, at the head of which were a dozen monks wearing colored habits, followed by a train of serious-looking notables wearing black dress and carrying a coffin. They marked the end of the formal funeral party and a teeming mass of people followed, without order or direction. The procession halted and one of the black-suited individuals appeared on a balcony — papers in hand: "It is our duty, as we say farewell to this great and worthy man, somebody or other…" etc. After his interminable babbling, the procession moved a block further and another darkly dressed character materialized on a balcony. "Somebody or other is dead, but the memory of his good deeds and his unblemished integrity..." etc. And so, poor old somebody or other crossed to his final resting place like this, pursued by the hate of his fellow villagers who on every street corner unburdened themselves of him in flooding words.

Then, another day's traveling in much the same manner as previous ones, and finally: CUZCO!

EL OMBLIGO
the navel!

The word that most perfectly describes the city of Cuzco is evocative. Intangible dust of another era settles on its streets, rising like the disturbed sediment of a muddy lake when you touch its bottom. But there are two or three Cuzcos, or it's better to say, two or three ways the city can be summoned. When Mama Ocllo dropped her golden wedge into the soil and it sank effortlessly, the first Incas knew this was the place selected by Viracocha to be the permanent home for his chosen ones, who had left behind their nomadic lives to come as *conquistadores* to their promised land. With nostrils flaring zealously for new horizons, they watched as their formidable empire grew, always looking beyond the feeble barrier of the surrounding mountains. And the converted nomads set to expanding Tahuantinsuyo, fortifying as they did so the center of their conquered territory — the navel of the world — Cuzco.* And here grew, as a necessary defense for the empire, the imposing Sacsahuamán, dominating the city from its heights and protecting the palaces and

---

*Mama Ocllo was the sister/wife of Manco Capac, the first Inca Emperor. According to the legend, the two were born simultaneously, rising up from Lake Titicaca, symbolizing unity and equality of masculine and feminine. Viracocha was the Inca Creator God. Tahuantinsuyo (four quarters) was the Inca world, of which Cuzco was the center.

temples from the wrath of the enemies of the empire. The vision of this Cuzco emerges mournfully from the fortress destroyed by the stupidity of illiterate Spanish *conquistadores*, from the violated ruins of the temples, from the sacked palaces, from the faces of a brutalized race. This is the Cuzco inviting you to become a warrior and to defend, club in hand, the freedom and the life of the Inca.

High above the city another Cuzco can be seen, displacing the destroyed fortress: a Cuzco with colored-tile roofs, its gentle uniformity interrupted by the cuppola of a baroque church; and as the city falls away it shows us only its narrow streets and its native inhabitants dressed in typical costume, all the local colors. This Cuzco invites you to be a hesitant tourist, to pass over things superficially and to relax into the beauty beneath a leaden winter sky.

And there is yet another Cuzco, a vibrant city whose monuments bear witness to the formidable courage of the warriors who conquered the region in the name of Spain, the Cuzco to be found in museums and libraries, in the church facades and in the clear, sharp features of the white chiefs who even today feel pride in the conquest. This is the Cuzco asking you to pull on your armor and, mounted on the ample back of a powerful horse, cleave a path through the defenseless flesh of a naked Indian flock whose human wall collapses and disappears beneath the four hooves of the galloping beast.

Each one of these Cuzcos can be admired separately, and to each one we dedicated a part of our stay.

the land of the incas

Cuzco is completely surrounded by mountains that signified less a defense than a danger for its Inca inhabitants, who, in order to defend themselves, built the immense mass of a fortress, Sacsahuamán. This version of the story, at least, satisfies the superficial inquirer, a version which for obvious reasons I cannot discount. It's possible, however, that the fortress constituted the initial nucleus of the great city. In the period immediately after abandoning nomadic life, when the Incas were barely more than an ambitious tribe and when defense against a numerically superior adversary stemmed from closely protecting the settled population, the walls of Sacsahuamán offered an ideal site. This double function of city and fortress explains some of the reasoning behind its construction, which doesn't make sense if its purpose was simply to repel an invading enemy, and much less so considering Cuzco lay defenseless on every other periphery. It is worth noting that the fortress is built in such a way that it controls the two steep valleys leading to the city. The serrated walls mean that when enemies attacked they could be held hostage on three flanks, and if they penetrated these defenses, they came up against a similar wall and then a third. The defenders have room to maneuver, enabling them to concentrate on their counterattack.

All this, and the subsequent glory of the city, creates the impression that the Quechua warriors were undefeated in the defense of their fortress against pounding enemies. Even though the fortifications are the expression of a highly inventive people, intuitive in mathematics, they seem to belong — in my view, at least — to belong to the pre-Inca stage of their civilization, a period before they learned to appreciate the comforts of a material life; being a sober race the Quechuas didn't achieve a level of cultural splendor, but they did make interesting advances in the fields of architecture and the arts. The continued success of the Quechua warriors drove enemy tribes each time further from Cuzco, and so leaving the secure confines of the fortress, that in any case could no longer contain their multiplying race, they spread down the neighboring valley along the stream whose waters they used. Highly conscious of their present glory, they turned their eyes to the past, in search of an explanation for their superiority. In honor of the memory of a god whose omnipotence had allowed them to rise to dominance, they created temples and the priest caste. In this way, expressing their greatness in stone, an imposing Cuzco grew, into the city eventually conquered by the Spaniards.

Even today, when the bestial rage of the conquering rabble can be seen in each of the acts taken to eternalize the conquest, and the Inca caste has long since vanished as a dominant power, their stone blocks stand enigmatically, impervious to the ravages of time. When the white troops sacked the already defeated city, attacking the Inca temples with unbridled fury, they unified their greed for the gold that covered the walls in perfect representations of Inti the Sun God with the sadistic pleasure of exchanging for the bereaved idol of a joyful people, the joyful and life-giving symbol of a grieving people. The temples to Inti were razed to their foundations or their walls were made to serve the ascent of the churches of the new religion: the cathedral was erected over the remains of a grand palace, and above the walls of the Temple of the Sun rose the Church of Santo Domingo, lesson and punishment from the proud conqueror. And yet every so often, the heart of America, shuddering with indignation, sends a nervous spasm through the gentle back of the Andes, and tumultuous shock waves assault the surface of the land. Three times the cuppola of proud Santo Domingo has collapsed from on high to the rhythm of broken bones and its worn walls have opened and fallen too. But the foundations they rest on are unmoved, the great blocks of the Temple of the Sun exhibit their gray stone indifferently; however colossal the disaster befalling its oppressor, not one of its huge rocks shifts from its place.

But Kon's revenge is meager in the face of the magnitude of the insult. The gray stones have grown tired of pleading with their protector gods for the destruction of the abhorrent conquering race, and now they simply show an inanimate exhaustion — useful only for provoking the admiring grunts of some or other tourist. What use was the patient labor of the Indians, builders of the Inca Roca Palace, subtle sculptors of stone angles, when faced with the impetuous actions of the white *conquistadores* and their knowledge of brick work, vaulting and rounded arches?

The anguished Indian, waiting for the terrible vengeance of his gods, saw instead a cloud of churches rise, erasing even the possibility of a proud past. The six-meter walls of the Inca Roca Palace, considered by the *conquistadores* to be useful only as weight bearers for their colonial palace, reflect in their perfect stone structures the cry of the defeated warrior.

But the race that created *Ollantay** left something more than the conglomeration of Cuzco as a monument to its grand past. Along the Vilcanota or Urubamba rivers, over more than a hundred kilometers, the signs of the Inca past are scattered. The most important of them are always in the heights of the mountains, where their fortresses were impenetrable and secure from surprise attack. After trekking for two long hours along a rough path we reached the peak of Pisac; arriving there as well, though long before us, were the swords of the Spanish soldiers, destroying Pisac's defenders, defenses and even its temple. Among the dispersed mass of disorganized stone, you can perceive that it was once a defensive construction; the place where Intiwatana stayed and where he caught and tied up the midday sun; and the dwellings of the priests. So little is left!

---

*An epic drama of the Inca General Ollanta, put to death for falling in love with an Inca princess.

Tracing the course of the Vilcanota and passing by some relatively unimportant sites, we reached Ollantaytambo, a vast fortress where Manco II* rose up in arms against the Spaniards, resisting Hernando Pizarro's troops and founding the minor dynasty of the Four Incas. This dynasty coexisted with the Spanish Empire until its last effeminate representative was assassinated in Cuzco's main square, on the orders of Viceroy Toledo.

A rocky hill no less than 100 meters high plunges suddenly to the Río Vilcanota. The fortress rests on top and its single vulnerable side, connected to its mountain neighbors by narrow paths, is guarded by stone defenses that easily impede the access of any attacking force similar in strength to the defenders. The lower part of the construction has a purely defensive purpose, its less steep areas split into some 20 easily defendable levels, making an attacker vulnerable to counterattack on each side. The upper part of the fortress contained the soldiers' quarters and is crowned by a temple which probably housed their loot, in the form of precious metal objects. But of all that, not even a memory remains, and even the massive stone blocks that made up the temple have been removed from their resting place.

Near Sacsahuamán, on the road returning to Cuzco, there's an example of typical Inca construction which, in our guide's opinion, was a bathing place for the Incas. This seemed a little strange to me, given the distance between the site and Cuzco, unless it was a ritual bathing place for the monarch only. The ancient Inca emperors (if this version is correct) must have had even tougher skins than their descendants because the water, though wonderful to drink, is extremely cold. The site, crowned with three deep trapezoidal recesses (whose form and purpose are unclear), is called Tambomachay and is at the entrance to the Valley of the Incas.

But the site whose archaeological and "touristic" significance

---

*Put on the Inca throne by Francisco Pizarro after helping to unseat Atahualpa, Manco II in turn fought the Spaniards. His first rebellion was crushed at Ollantaytambo in 1536.

overwhelms all others in the region is Machu Picchu, which in the indigenous language means Old Mountain. The name is completely divorced from the settlement which sheltered within its hold the last members of a free people. For Bingham, the [U.S.] archaeologist who discovered the ruins, the place was more than a refuge against invaders, but was the original settlement of the dominant Quechua race and a sacred site for them. Later, in the period of the Spanish conquest, it also became a hideout for the defeated army. At first glance there are several indications that the above-mentioned archaeologist was right. In Ollantaytambo, for example, the most important defensive constructions face away from Machu Picchu, even though the slope behind is not steep enough to ensure effective defense against attack from there, possibly suggesting that their backs were covered in that direction. A further indication is their preoccupation with keeping the area hidden from outsiders, even after all resistance had been crushed. The last Inca himself was captured far from Machu Picchu, where Bingham found skeletons that were almost all female, which he identified as being those of virgins of the Temple of the Sun, a religious order whose members the Spaniards never managed to flush out. As is customary in constructions like this, the Temple of the Sun with its famous Intiwatana crowns the city. It is carved from the rock which also serves as its pedestal, and close by a series of carefully polished stones suggest that this is a very important place. Looking out across the river are three trapezoidal windows typical of Quechua architecture, which Bingham identified as the windows through which the Ayllus brothers in Inca mythology came to the outside world to show the chosen people the path to their promised land. To my understanding the idea is a little strained. The interpretation has, of course, been contested by a great many prestigious researchers. There is also voluminous debate about the function of the Temple of the Sun whose discoverer, Bingham, maintained it was a circular enclosure, similar to the temple dedicated to the same sun god in Cuzco. Whatever the case, the form and cut of the stones suggest it was of principal importance, and it is thought that beneath the huge stones that form the temple's base lies the tomb of the Inca or Incas.

Here you can easily appreciate the difference between the different social classes of the village, each of them occupying a distinct place according to their grouping, and remaining more or less independent from the rest of the community. It's a pity they knew no other roofing matter besides straw; now there are no examples of roofing left, even on the most luxurious sites. But for architects who had no knowledge of vaulting or arch supports, it must have been very difficult to resolve this problem. In the buildings reserved for the warriors, we were shown cavities in the stone walls, like small chambers, and on either side of them holes just big enough for a man's arm to pass through had been hollowed out. This was apparently a place of physical punishment; the victim was forced to place both arms through the respective holes and was then pushed backwards until his bones broke. I was unconvinced about the effectiveness of the procedure and introduced my limbs in the manner indicated. Alberto pushed me slowly: the slight pressure provoked excruciating pain and the sensation that I would be torn apart completely if he continued to press my chest.

But you can really appreciate the imposing magnitude of the city-fortress from the view at Huayna Picchu (Young Mountain), rising some 200 meters higher. The place must have been used as a kind of lookout point rather than as housing or as fortifications because the ruins are only of minor importance. Machu Picchu is impregnable on two of its sides, defended by an abyss dropping a sheer 300 meters to the river and a narrow gorge linking up with the "young mountain"; its most vulnerable side is defensible from a succession of terraces making any attack against it extremely difficult, while to Machu Picchu's face, looking approximately south, vast fortifications and the natural narrowing of the hilltop make a difficult pass through which to attack. If you remember also that the torrential Vilcanota rushes around the base of the mountain, you can see that the first inhabitants of Machu Picchu were wise in their choice.

In reality it hardly matters what the primitive origins of the city are. It's best, in any case, to leave discussion of the subject to arch-aeologists. The most important and irrefutable thing, however, is that here we found the pure expression of the most powerful indig-enous race in the Americas — still clean of contact with a conquer-ing civilization and replete with immensely evocative treasures bet-ween its walls that have died from the tedium of having no life between them. The spectacular landscape circling the fortress supp-lies an essential backdrop, inspiring dreamers to wander its ruins for the sake of it; North American tourists, bound down by their practical world view, are able to place those members of the disinte-grating tribes they may have seen in their travels among these once-living walls, unaware of the moral distance separating them, since only the semi-indigenous spirit of the South American can grasp the subtle differences.

EL SEÑOR DE LOS TEMBLORES
lord of the earthquakes

From the cathedral, the peals of the María Angola rung out for the first time since the earthquake. Legend has it that this famous bell, among the largest in the world, contains 27 kilograms of gold. It was supposedly donated by a lady called María Angulo, but the name of the bell itself was changed due to a slight problem with rhyming slang.*

The cost of restoring the cathedral bell towers, destroyed by the earthquake of 1950, had been met by General Franco's government,** and as a gesture of gratitude the band was ordered to play the Spanish national anthem. As the first chords sounded, the bishop's red headdress locked itself into position as he moved his arms about like a puppet. "Stop, stop, there's been a mistake," he whispered, while the indignant voice of a Spaniard could be heard, "Two years' work, and they play this!" I couldn't say whether with good intentions or otherwise, the band had struck up the Spanish Republican anthem.

In the afternoon he leaves his stately home in the cathedral, Our Lord of the Earthquakes, who is no more than a dark brown image of Christ. He is paraded throughout the city and his pilgrimage stops at all the main churches. As he passes, a crowd of layabouts competes with each other to throw handfuls of the little flowers that grow abundantly on the slopes of the nearby mountains, named by the natives *nucchu*. The violent red of the flowers, the intense bronze of the Lord of the Earthquakes and the silver altar they carry him on lend the procession the impression that it's a pagan festival, a feeling that is intensified by the many-colored clothes of the Indians, who wear for the occasion their best traditional costumes in expression of a culture or way of life which still holds on to living values. In contrast, a cluster of Indians in European clothes march at the head of the procession, carrying banners. Their tired, affected faces resemble an image of those Quechuas who refused to heed Manco II's call, pledging themselves to Pizarro and in the degradation of their defeat smothering the pride of an independent race.

Standing over the small frames of the Indians gathered to see the procession pass, the blond head of a North American can occa-

*Because it rhymed with *culo* (ass in Spanish).
**General Franco was military dictator in Spain from 1936 until his death in 1975.

sionally be glimpsed, who, with his camera and sports shirt, seems to be (and, in fact, actually is) a correspondent from another world lost amid the isolation of the Inca Empire.

EL SOLAR DEL VENCEDOR
homeland for the victor

What was once the lavish capital of the Inca Empire conserved much of its brilliance for many years — out of simple inertia. There were new men flaunting its riches, but they were the same riches. For a time they were not merely maintained but augmented, with the products of the gold and silver mines that converged on the region; the sole difference being that Cuzco no longer bore the title "navel of the world" but was just another point on its periphery. Its treasures emigrated to the new metropolis across the sea to feed the opulence of another imperial court. The Indians no longer worked with determination at the barren soil; yet the *conquistadores* had not come to fight daily with the land for their sustenance, but to gain easy fortunes through heroic deeds or simple greed. Slowly Cuzco languished, pushed to the margins, lost in the cordillera, while on the Pacific coast a new rival emerged, Lima, growing with the fruits of the taxes levied by clever intermediaries on the wealth flowing out of Peru. Although there was no cataclysm by which to mark the transition, the brilliant Inca capital passed into its current state, a relic of times gone by. Only recently has one or other modern building arisen to clash with the existing collection, but otherwise all the monuments of colonial splendor still remain.

The cathedral is grounded firmly in the center of the city. Its solidity, typical to its era, makes it look more like a fortress than a church. The glitz of its brilliant interior reflects a glorious past; the giant paintings reposing on the lateral walls do not measure up to riches scattered through the sanctuary but somehow they do not seem out of place, and a St. Christopher emerging from the water seemed, at least to me, a fine piece. The earthquake wreaked havoc there as well: the frames of the paintings are broken and the paintings themselves scratched and creased. The effect created by the golden frames and the golden doors to the side altars all falling off their hinges is very strange, as if they're revealing the lesions of age. Gold doesn't have the gentle dignity of silver which becomes more charming as it ages, and so the cathedral seems to be decorated like an old woman with too much makeup. There is real artistry in the choir stalls, made from wood by Indian or mestizo craftsmen. In their carved scenes of the lives of the saints, they have infused the cedar with the spirit of the Catholic Church and the enigmatic soul of the true Andean peoples.

One of Cuzco's jewels, worthy of the visits by each and every tourist, is the pulpit of the Basilica of San Blas. It has nothing more to show for itself except the fine carving, before which you pause, enraptured, and like the choir stalls of the cathedral it expresses the fusion of two hostile but somehow almost complementary races. The whole city is an immense gallery: the churches, of course, but even every house, every balcony looking out over every street, is like a medium with which to evoke times past. Each of those is not with the same merit, of course. But as I write in this moment, so far from there, when my notes before me seem faded and artificial, I'm unable to say which impressed me the most. Amid the magma of churches we visited I remember the pitiful image of the bell towers of the Church of Belén, toppled by the earthquake, lying like a dismembered animal on the hillside.

After careful analysis, there are very few works of art capable of standing up under close inspection; Cuzco is not a city to visit for this or that painting. Rather, it's the whole of the city together which creates the impression of the peaceful, if sometimes disquieting, center of a civilization that has long since passed.

CUZCO A SECAS
cuzco straight

If everything that goes to make up Cuzco were erased from the face of the earth and in its place a little, history-less village appeared, there would still always be something to say about it. As if mixing cocktails, we threw all our impressions together. Our life in those two weeks never lost the hobo character marking our whole journey. The letter of introduction we had for Dr. Hermosa turned out to be fairly useful, although in actual fact he was not the type of man who needed such a formal presentation to lend a hand. It was enough for him to know Alberto had worked with Dr. Fernández, one of the most eminent leprologists in the Americas, and Alberto brandished the card with his customary skill. Extensive discussion with Dr. Hermosa gave us an approximate picture of Peruvian life and the opportunity to make a trip around the entire Valley of the Incas in his car. He was very kind to us and was also the one who found us train tickets to Machu Picchu.

The average speed of the regional trains is about 10 to 20 kilometers an hour — such consumptive conditions achieved by being constantly affronted with considerable climbs and descents. In order that trains might win against the difficult ascent as they leave the city, the tracks had to be constructed in such a way that the train moves forward for a while, then slips backwards to another track from where it begins a new climb, and this back and forth is repeated several times until it reaches to the top and begins its descent along the course of a river which eventually flows into the Vilcanota. On the train trip we met a pair of Chilean swindlers, selling herbs and telling fortunes. They were very friendly toward us, sharing their food after we had invited them to drink our *mate*. On reaching the ruins, we stumbled across a group of footballers and were invited to play. I had the opportunity to show off a few impressive catches, before humbly admitting that I'd played premier league football in Buenos Aires with Alberto, who demonstrated his skill in midfield on a pitch the locals call a *pampa*. Our relatively spectacular flair gained us the attention of the owner of the ball who was also the manager of the hotel. He invited us to stay a couple of days there, until the next gang of North Americans were shipped in on their special rail coaches. Señor Soto, as well as being a wonderful individual, was also a very learned person and after exhausting his favorite topic of sport we were able to speak at length about Inca culture, about which he knew a great deal.

We felt pretty sad when the moment came to leave. We drank the last exquisite coffee prepared by Señora Soto and boarded the little train for its 12-hour trip back to Cuzco. In these types of trains there are third-class carriages "reserved" for the local Indians: they're like the cattle transportation wagons they use in Argentina, except that the smell of cow shit is ever more pleasant than the human version. The somewhat animal-like concept the indigenous people have of modesty and hygiene means that irrespective of gender or age they do their business by the roadside, the women cleaning themselves with their skirts, the men not bothering at all, and then carry on as before. The underskirts of Indian women who have kids are literally warehouses of excrement, a consequence of the way they wipe the rascals every time one of them passes wind. Of course, the tourists traveling in their comfortable rail coaches could only glean the vaguest idea of the conditions in which the Indians live, from the fast glimpses they catch as they speed past our train, which has stopped to let them pass. The fact that it was the U.S. archaeologist Bingham who discovered the ruins and expounded his findings in easily accessible articles for the general public, means that Machu Picchu is by now very famous in that country to the north and the majority of North Americans visiting Peru come here (in general they fly direct to Lima, tour Cuzco, visit the ruins and return straight home, not believing that anything else is worth seeing).

The archaeological museum in Cuzco is pretty poor. When the authorities opened their eyes to the mountain of treasure being smuggled out of the various sites, it was already too late. Treasure hunters, tourists, foreign archaeologists, anyone at all with any interest in the subject, had systematically looted the region and they were able to collect for the museum only what remained: virtually the scraps. Even so, for people like us, without much of an archaeo-logical education and with only muddled and recently acquired knowledge of Inca civilization, there was enough to see, and we saw it over several days. The mestizo curator was very knowledge-able with a breathtaking enthusiasm for the race whose blood flow-ed in his veins. He spoke to us of the splendid past and the present misery, of the urgent need to educate the Indians, as a first step toward total rehabilitation. He insisted that immediately raising the economic level of Indian families was the only way to mitigate the soporific effects of coca and drink and talked of fostering a fuller and more exact understanding of the Quechua people so that indi-viduals of that race could look at their past and feel pride, rather than, looking at their present, feel only shame at belonging to the Indian or mestizo class. At that time the coca problem was being debated in the United Nations and we told him about our experience with the drug and its effects. He replied that the same had happened to him, and exploded with a string of abuse against those who make profits from poisoning large numbers of people. The Colla and Quechua races form the majority in Peru and are the only ones who consume coca. The semi-indigenous features of the curator, his eyes shining with enthusiasm and his faith in the future, constituted one more treasure of the museum, but a living museum, proof of a race still fighting for its identity.

HUAMBO
huambo

Our source of doorbells dried up and following Gardel's advice we turned to face the north.* Abancay was a forced stop because from there the trucks left for Huancarama, the last town before the leper colony at Huambo. Our preferred method of soliciting bed and board didn't change at all from before (Civil Guard and hospital), neither did that for transportation — hitching a lift — except that for the latter we had to wait two days because no trucks departed during the days of Easter. We wandered aimlessly around the little village, finding nothing particularly interesting, not enough to forget our hunger, with the hospital food being so scarce. Lying in a field next to stream, we looked at the sky, changing with evening, dreaming up old memories of past loves, or picturing in every cloud the tempting image of ordinary food.

*Carlos Gardel was a famous Argentine actor and composer of tangos.

Returning to the police station for some sleep, we took a short cut and lost our way completely. We made our way through fields and over fences, eventually coming to rest on the porch of a house. We had already climbed the stone wall when we saw a dog and his owner, illuminated by the full moon, looking like ghosts! But we didn't realize that our figures, outlined against the night, would have been much more terrifying. In response to my polite "good evening" we heard only unintelligible noise — I think I caught the word "Viracocha!"* — and then man and dog fled into the house ignoring our apologies and friendly calls. We left, calmly, by the front gate leading on to a path which seemed more like the right way.

In one of those moments of boredom we went to the church to watch up close a little local ceremony. The poor priest was attempting a three-hour sermon but by then — an hour and a half into it — he had exhausted his stock of maxims. He looked over the congregation, his eyes pleading, while with his hands he pointed desperately to different parts of the church. "Look, look, the Lord has come to us, the Lord is among us and His spirit guides us." After a moment's truce, the priest set off on another tangent and just when it seemed he would hold his silence — a moment of high drama — he sent himself off again into similar nonsense. The fifth or sixth time that a patient Christ was introduced, we got an attack of hysterics and left hurriedly.

What exactly brought on an asthma attack I can't say (though I can guess one of the faithful does), but by the time we arrived in Huancarama I could hardly stand on my feet. I had no adrenalin and my asthma worsened. Wrapped in a police blanket, I watched the rain and smoked one black cigarette after another, which helped to relieve the fatigue somewhat. Somewhere near dawn I managed to fall asleep, leaning against a pillar in the hallway. By the morning I felt a little better and Alberto found some adrenalin, which

*Inca Creator God. The term is sometimes also used by Indians for white people.

along with some aspirin left me feeling like new.

We notified the lieutenant governor, a sort of village mayor, of our presence and to ask him for a couple of horses to take us to the leper colony. The very friendly man attended to us happily, promising that in five minutes we'd have horses waiting for us at the police station. As we waited for the animals, we stopped to watch a motley group of guys exercising to the domineering commands of the soldier who'd been so kind to us just the day before. On seeing us arrive, he saluted us with great deference, then continued delivering his orders for every type of drill to the clowns in his charge. Only one out of every five young men of eligible age completes military service in Peru, but the rest are submitted to drills each Sunday and these were the soldier's victims we were witnessing. In fact, they were all victims: the conscripts, of the wrath of their instructor, and he of his pupils' sluggishness. Not understanding most of his Spanish; not grasping the fundamental importance of turning this way, then that; or of marching then stopping at the whim of their boss, they did everything halfheartedly and were enough to make anyone get angry.

The horses arrived and the soldier allotted us a guide who spoke nothing but Quechua. The route began with a mountainous track which no other horses would have been able to cross, preceded by the guide on foot who took the horses' bridles in difficult sections. We'd covered about two-thirds of the distance when an old woman and a boy appeared. They grabbed our reins and launched into a lengthy tirade of which we recognized a word sounding like "horse." We thought at first they were selling cane baskets because the old woman was carrying a good many. "Me no want buy, me no want," I kept saying to her, and would have continued in that vein if Alberto hadn't reminded me that our interlocutors were Quechua, not relatives of Tarzan and the Apes. We finally found a person coming from the opposite direction who spoke Spanish who explained to us that these Indians were the owners of the horses;

that they were riding past the front of the lieutenant governor's house when he had taken their horses and presented them to us. One of the conscripts, the owner of my horse, had come seven leagues to comply with his military duty, and the old and poor woman lived in the opposite direction to that we were heading in. We did what any decent person would do — dismounted, and continued along the road on foot, the guide ahead of us hauling all our things on his back. We completed the last stretch to the leper colony like this, where we gave our guide one *sol* in recompense. He thanked us profusely, despite it being such a pathetic amount.

The head of the clinic, Señor Montejo, received us, and though he couldn't put us up he said he'd send us to the home of one of the region's landowners, which is exactly what he did. The rancher gave us a room with beds and food, all that we needed. The following morning we went to pay a visit to the patients in the little hospital. The people who are in charge do a great job, even if it goes unnoticed. The general state of the place is disastrous; two-thirds of a small area — the size of less than half a block — is designated as a "sick zone," and in it the entire lives of the 31 condemned take place. They pass the time watching indifferently for death to arrive (at least that's what I think). Sanitary conditions are appalling, and though this might cause no adverse effects on the Indians from the mountains, people coming from other parts, even if only slightly more educated, find it enormously distressing. The thought of having to spend their whole lives between four adobe walls, surrounded by people speaking another language, with only four orderlies who make just short visits each day, causes nervous breakdowns.

We went into a room with a straw roof, its ceiling slatted with cane and an earth floor where a white girl was reading *Cousin Basilio* by Queirós. No sooner had we begun to talk when the girl broke down, crying inconsolably, describing her life as a "calvary," a living hell. The poor girl, from the Amazonian regions, had gone to Cuzco where they gave her the bad news, and said they would send her to a much better place to be cured. The hospital in Cuzco, by no means perfect, did have a certain level of comfort. I believe her expression, the word "calvary," was the only just expression for the girl's situation. The only acceptable thing in this hospital was the drug treatment, the rest could have been borne only by the suffering, fatalistic spirit of the Peruvian mountain Indians.

The imbecility of the neighboring locals only heightened the isolation of both patients and medical staff. One of them told us that the head surgeon at the clinic needed to perform a more or less serious operation, impossible at any rate to execute on a kitchen table and lacking the appropriate surgical equipment. So he asked for a place, even if it was the morgue, in a nearby hospital at Andahuaylas. The answer was negative, and the patient died without treatment. Señor Montejo told us that when this leprosy treatment center was founded, on the initiative of the renowned leprologist Dr. Pesce, he himself had been responsible, from the center's inception, for organizing new services. When he arrived in the town Huancarama, not one of the hostels or hotels would let him a room for the night; the one or two friends he had in town refused to give him shelter and in light of the fact that rain was looming, he had been forced to seek refuge in a pigsty, where he passed the night. The patient I spoke of earlier had to walk to the leper colony because there was no one who would lend her and her companion horses — this was years after the colony had been founded.

After welcoming us in great style, they took us to see a new hospital going up a few kilometers from the old one. As they asked for our opinions, the orderlies' eyes shone proudly, as if the building was their own creation, built adobe brick by adobe brick through their own sweat. It seemed a little heartless to emphasize our criticisms. But the new leper colony has the same disadvantages as the old: it lacks a laboratory, it lacks surgical facilities and, to exacerbate matters, it's situated in an area infested by mosquitoes, representing pure torture for anyone who has to spend a whole day there. Yes, it's capable of housing 250 patients, a resident doctor and it has made some advances in hygiene, but there is still a lot to do.

After two days' stay in the region, in which my asthma worsened, we decided to leave and try to get some proper treatment further on.

With horses provided by the rancher who had given us lodging, we set off on the return journey, accompanied by the same laconic Quechua-speaking guide who carried our bags at the landowner's insistence. In the mentality of the district's rich people it's perfectly natural that the servant, although traveling on foot, should carry all the weight and discomfort. We waited until the first bend erased us from sight and took our bags from our guide, whose enigmatic face revealed nothing of whether or not he appreciated the gesture.

We again stayed with the Civil Guard back in Huancarama, until finding a truck to take us further in our determined northward direction, which we secured the next day. After an exhausting day of travel, we finally arrived in the town of Andahuaylas, and I went straight to the hospital to recover.

SIEMPRE AL NORTE
ever northward

After resting for two days in the hospital, and partly recovered, we abandoned that refuge to once again accept the charity of our great friends the Civil Guard, who received us with good humor as usual. We were so short on money we were almost scared to eat; but we didn't want to work until reaching Lima where there was the reasonable hope we'd find better paid work and save enough to continue on the road, since there was still no talk of turning back.

The first night's wait passed well enough because the lieutenant in charge of the post, an accommodating type, invited us to eat, and we ate enough to store up for whatever lay ahead. Only hunger, however, by now a daily companion, marked the following two days, and boredom; it was impossible to go very far from the checkpoint since the truck drivers inevitably had to go there to get their papers checked, before beginning or continuing their journeys.

At the end of the third day, our fifth in Andahuaylas, we found what we'd been waiting for in the form of a truck heading to Ayacucho. Just in time, it turned out, because Alberto had reacted violently on seeing Civil Guard soldiers insulting an Indian woman who had come to bring food to her imprisoned husband. His reaction must have seemed completely alien to people who considered the Indians were no more than objects, who deserve to live but only just. After that, we fell out of favor.

With night falling, we left the village in whose obligatory hiatus we had been prisoners for several days. The truck now had to climb to the peak of the mountains guarding the northerly exit from Andahuaylas, and it got colder by the minute. To top it off, we were completely drenched by one of the violent regional rainstorms and this time we had no defense against it, installed as we were in the tray of a truck taking 10 young bulls to Lima and charged with their care, together with an Indian boy who was also the driver's helper. We all spent the night in a town named Chincheros. As for ourselves, so cold we had forgotten we were also pariahs, without money, we ate a very modest meal and asked for one bed for both of us. Our request was accompanied, needless to say, by many tears and lamentations that must have moved the owner somewhat: five *soles* for everything. We spent the whole next day passing from deep ravines to the "pampas," as they call the tablelands on top of the mountain chains throughout Peru. The country's irregular topography knows almost no plains at all, save for the forested regions of the Amazon. Our job increased in difficulty with the passing of the hours, since the animals, having lost the layer of sawdust they had been standing on, and tired of waiting in the same position absorbing the jolts of the truck, started falling over. We had to get them back on their feet, because of the danger that an animal trampled by the others might die.

At one particular moment Alberto thought that the horn of one animal was scraping the eye of another and told the young Indian who was close to the action. With a shrug of his shoulders, into which he poured the whole spirit of his race, he said, "Why, when all it'll ever see is shit," and quietly continued tying a knot, the task he'd been dedicated to before being interrupted.

We finally arrived in Ayacucho, famous in Latin American history for the decisive battle Bolívar won on the plains circumscribing the town. The terrible street lighting plaguing the whole of the Peruvian sierra reached its worst there; the electric lights emit only the slightest orange glow which shines throughout the night. A gentleman, whose hobby it was to collect foreign friends, invited us to sleep at his house and the next day found for us a truck heading north, so we could only visit one or two of the 33 churches the little town holds within its urban boundaries. We said farewell to our good friend and set off again for Lima.

through the center of peru

Our journey continued in much the same way, eating now and then whenever some generous soul took pity on our indigence. Still, we never ate very much and the deficit became even graver when we were told that evening there had been a landslide further ahead and we couldn't pass; we would have to spend the night in a little village called Anco. Early the next day we set off again, mounted on our truck, but only a little way up the road we reached the landslide and had to spend the day there, starving and curious, observing the workers set explosives to the huge boulders that had fallen on the road. For every laborer, there were no less than five bossy supervisors, shouting out their opinions and hindering the work of the dynamiters, who were not exactly model workers themselves.

We tried to fool our hunger by going down to swim in the torrential river running through the gully below, but the water was too icy to stay in for long and neither of us is particularly resistant to the cold, as I've said before. In the end, after one of our stock stories of woe, one of the men gave us some corn cobs and another a cow's heart and some offal.

A woman loaned us her pot and we began to organize our meal, but halfway through the task the dynamiters freed the road and the troupe of trucks began to move. The woman took back her pot and we had to eat the corn uncooked and put away the raw meat. To cap off our misery, night was closing in and a terrible rainstorm transformed the road into a dangerous river of mud. There was only room for one truck at a time, so those on the far side of the landslide came through first, followed by those on our side. We were among the first in a long line, but the differential on the very first truck broke when pushed too violently by the tractor assisting in the hard crossings, and we were all blocked again. Finally, a jeep with a pulley on the front came down from the other side of the hill, hauling the truck to the side of the road, allowing the rest of us to continue on our way. The vehicle drove through the night and as usual we went from more or less sheltered valleys on to those frigid Peruvian pampas where we were stabbed by the ice and driving rain. Our teeth chattered, Alberto's and mine, from the chill caused by sitting in the same position, and we took turns to stretch our legs to stop them cramping. Our hunger was a like a strange animal, living not just in one particular part but all over our bodies, making us nervous and bad tempered.

We arrived in Huancallo with first light breaking and walked the 15 blocks from where the truck dropped us to the Civil Guard post, our regular stopover. We bought some bread, made *mate* and were beginning to take out our famous raw heart and offal but had not even stoked up the embers of a recently made fire when a truck heading to Oxapampa offered us a ride. Our interest in going to the place stemmed from the fact that the mother of one of our Argentine *compañeros* lived there, at least we thought she did. We were holding on to the hope that she might help kill our hunger for a few days and perhaps even adorn us with a *sol* or two. So we left Huancallo almost without seeing it, motivated by the eager cries of our exhausted stomachs.

The first part of the road was wonderful, passing through a little group of towns, but by six in the evening we had begun a perilous descent down an extremely narrow road, good enough for only one vehicle at a time. It was generally the case that only traffic coming from one direction was permitted to pass on any given day, but for some unknown reason they had made this day an exception, and the trucks negotiated their crossings, shouting profusely and tightly maneuvering; their rear wheels inching out over the precipitous edges — not exactly a calming spectacle.

Alberto and I crouched in each corner of the truck, ready to jump for solid ground at the first sign of any accident, but our Indian traveling companions didn't move a muscle. Our fears were based in fact, however, since a good many crosses punctuating this part of the mountainous coast mark the mishaps of less fortunate colleagues among the drivers using the route. And every truck that ran off the road took its tremendous human cargo with it, down the 200-meter abyss to the seething river below — laying waste to any hope of survival. Every single accident, according to regional accounts, had left every single person dead — not a sole injured survivor.

This time, luckily, nothing unpleasant happened and at about 10 at night we reached a village by the name of La Merced. It rested in a low-lying, tropical area and had the typical look of any jungle village. Another charitable soul ceded us a bed for the night and a huge meal. The meals were included at the last moment when the man came to see if we were okay and we had no time to hide the peel of some oranges we had picked from some tree to try and calm our hunger.

In the town's Civil Guard post we learned unhappily that trucks didn't have to stop to register, making it very hard to hitch any rides. While there, we witnessed the reporting of a murder, by the victim's son and an ostentatious mulatto who said he was an intimate friend of the dead man. The act had mysteriously occurred some days earlier, and the prime suspect was an Indian whose photo the two men had brought with them. The sergeant showed it to us, saying, "Look, doctors, the classic image of a murderer." We nodded enthusiastically, but on leaving the station I asked Alberto, "Which one exactly is the murderer?" And his thinking was much the same as mine, that the dark guy had a much more murderous aspect than the Indian.

In the long hours waiting for our ride, we made friends with someone who said he could arrange everything and that it would cost us nothing. True to his word, he spoke with a truck driver who agreed to take us. It turned out later, however, that he had merely organized that each of us would pay five *soles* less than the 20 per head the driver usually charged. We pleaded that we were completely broke, which was only a few cents away from being the truth. He promised to meet the debt, and this he did, taking us home for the night as well, after we arrived.

The road was fairly narrow, though not nearly as bad as the previous one, and pretty, winding through forest or tropical fruit plantation: bananas, papayas and others. It climbed up and down the whole way to Oxapampa, some 1,000 meters above sea level, which was our destination and the end of the highway.

Until this point we had been traveling in the same truck as the black guy who had reported the murder. At one of the stops along the road he bought us a meal and throughout it, lectured us on coffee, papaya and the black slaves, of whom his grandfather had been one. He said this quite openly but it you could detect a note of shame in his voice. In any case, Alberto and I agreed to absolve him of any guilt in the murder of his friend.

ESPERANZA FALLIDA
shattered hopes

With great disgust we learned the following morning that our Argentine friend had given us bad information and his mother hadn't lived in Oxapampa for quite a long time. A brother-in-law lived there instead, so he had to deal with our dead weight. The reception was magnificent and we had a big, improvised meal, but we soon realized that as guests we were only welcome out of traditional Peruvian courtesy. We decided to ignore everything besides express marching orders, seeing as we were completely out of money and had built up several days worth of hunger, and as we could eat only consistently in the home of our disinclined friends.

We had what for us was a wonderful day; swimming in the river, letting all of our worries disappear, eating a lot of good food and drinking exquisite coffee. But all good things sadly come to an end and by nightfall of the second day, the engineer (our "host" was an engineer) came up with a formula for his own salvation which was not only effective but particularly cheap: some roads inspector had offered to take us all the way to Lima. It seemed like a great idea to us as we were acutely feeling the restricted horizons and wanted to get to the capital to try and improve our luck. In other words, we fell for it, hook, line and sinker.

That night we boarded the back of a pickup truck which, after we had endured a violent downpour soaking us to our bones, dropped us at two in the morning in San Ramón, much less than even halfway to Lima. The driver said we should wait while he changed vehicles and to calm any suspicions he left his companion with us. After 10 minutes that guy went off to buy cigarettes, and at five in the morning this pair of Argentine wise guys breakfasted on the bitter realization that we had been taken for one long ride.

All I hope is that the driver gets what he deserves, and that, if it wasn't another one of his lies, the driver-come-torero meets death on the horns of one of his bulls… (In the pit of my stomach I knew something was wrong but he seemed like such a nice person that we believed everything... even the whole vehicle swap.)

Shortly before dawn, we came across a couple of drunks and did our brilliant "anniversary" routine. The technique is as follows:

1. Say something loudly, immediately identifiable as Argentine, something with a *che* in it and other bits of slang and drawl. The candidate takes the bait, immediately asking where we're from;

we strike up a conversation.

2. Begin to speak of the hardships but don't make too much of them, all the while maintaining a gaze fixed in the distance.

3. I intervene and ask for the date; someone provides it and Alberto sighs, saying: "Imagine the coincidence, it was a year ago today." The candidate asks, a year ago since what; we respond that it was when we began our journey.

4. Alberto, much bolder than I am, lets out a gigantic sigh, saying, "Such a pity we're in these dire circumstances, we aren't able to celebrate" (he says this quietly, as if confiding in me). The candidate immediately offers to pay; we pretend to refuse for a while, admitting it would be impossible for us to ever pay him back, etc., and then finally, we accept the offer.

5. After the first drink, I steadfastly refuse to accept another and Alberto makes a face at me. Our host becomes a little angry and insists, but I refuse, without giving reasons. The man asks and asks until I confess, full of embarrassment, that our custom in Argentina is to eat when we drink. Just how much we eat depends on how we judge the candidate's face. All in all, this is a highly refined technique.

In San Ramón we tried it again and, as always, were able to concretize the enormous amount we had to drink with some solid food. In the morning we rested on the shores of the river — a very pretty landscape even though its beauty escaped our aesthetic attentions somewhat, transforming itself into terrifying mirages of all types of edible delicacies. Nearby, peeking through a fence, the plump forms of oranges materialized. Our feast was fierce and sad; in one minute our stomachs felt full and acidy and in the next the stabbing of a severe hunger resumed.

Famished, we decided to cast off the little shame that stubbornly remained, and to sort ourselves out at the local hospital. This time it was Alberto who was overcome with a strange timidity, and I had to find the right words to intone the following diplomatic speech:

"Doctor" — we found one in the hospital — "I am a medical student, my companion is a biochemist. The both of us are from Argentina and we are hungry. We would like to eat." In such a surprise frontal attack, the poor doctor could do nothing but agree to buy us a meal from the restaurant where he himself ate. We were so brazen.

Alberto was so ashamed he didn't even thank him, and we set about fishing for another truck, which we eventually caught. We were now heading to Lima, comfortably installed in the driver's cabin, who now and then even paid for coffee.

We were climbing the extremely narrow mountain road which had inspired such fear on the way in. The driver was happily relating the history of each and every cross lining the way, when suddenly he hit a huge hole in the middle of the road, visible to any fool. Our dread that the man didn't know how to drive crept steadily higher, but elementary logic told us this wasn't possible, that on this road anyone but the most experienced of drivers would have driven over the edge long ago. Tactfully and with patience, Alberto extracted the real story. The man had been in an accident which, according to him, had left his eyesight very poor, explaining why he hit so many potholes. We tried to make him understand the dangers — for him, and for the people traveling with him. But the driver was unyielding: this was his job, and he was paid very well by a boss who didn't ask *how* he arrived, only *if* he arrived. Besides, his driving license had been very expensive, in light of the decent bribe he'd had to pay to get it.

The owner of the truck climbed on board a little further down the road. He seemed happy to take us to Lima but only if I, riding up top, would hide away when we came to police checkpoints because taking passengers on freight trucks like this one was prohibited. The owner also turned out to be a good person, giving us food all the way to the capital. We passed through La Oroya before that, however, a mining town we dearly wanted to see, but we weren't able to stop. La Oroya is at an altitude of some 4,000 meters, and from its unrefined appearance you can picture the hardship in a miner's life. Its tall chimneys throw up black smoke, impregnating everything with soot, and the miners' faces as they traveled the streets were also imbued with that ancient melancholy of smoke, unifying everything with its grayish monotones, a perfect coupling with the gray mountain days. We crossed the highest point on the road while it was still light, at 4,853 meters above sea level. Though it was still daytime, the cold was intense. Tucked up in my traveling blanket, staring out at the view extending on every side, I muttered all sorts of verses, lulled by the roar of the truck.

That night we slept just outside the city, and the following day we made it early to Lima.

LA CIUDAD DE LOS VIRREYES
the city of the viceroys

We were at the end of one of the most important stages of our journey, without a cent or much chance in the short term of making any money, but we were happy.

Lima is a pretty city, which has already suppressed its colonial past (after seeing Cuzco it seems more so) beneath new houses. Its fame as a precious jewel of a city is unjustified, but its residential suburbs are connected by wide avenues to the extremely agreeable resorts close to the sea. The people of Lima travel from the city to the port of Callao along various wide arterials in just a few minutes. The port has no special attraction (construction of all ports seems to be completely standardized) save the fort, the scene of many battles. Alongside its enormous walls we stood in wonder at Lord Cochrane's extraordinary feat when, leading his Latin American sailors, he attacked and seized this bastion in one of the most celebrated episodes in the history of Latin America's liberation.

The part of Lima really worth describing is the city center around its wonderful cathedral, so different from that heavy monstrosity in Cuzco, where the *conquistadores* crudely glorified themselves. There in Lima, the art is more stylized, with an almost effeminate touch: the cathedral towers are tall and graceful, maybe the most slender of all the cathedrals in the Spanish colonies. The lavishness of the woodwork in Cuzco has been left behind and taken up here in gold. The naves are light and airy, contrasting with those dark, hostile caverns of the Inca city. The paintings are also bright, almost joyous, and of schools more recent than the hermetic mestizos, who painted their saints with a dark and captive fury. All of the churches convey in their facades and altars the full scope of Churrigueresque gold-embellished art.* This vast wealth enabled the aristocracy to resist the liberating armies of America until the last moment. Lima is the perfect example of a Peru which has not developed beyond the feudal condition of a colony. It still waits for the blood of a truly emancipating revolution.

But there is a corner of the regal city which is most dear to us, and we went there frequently to relive our memories of Machu Picchu; this was the Museum of Archaeology and Anthropology. Don Julio Tello was its creator, a pure blood Indian scholar. It contains extremely valuable collections, synthesizing entire cultures.

Lima is quite unlike Córdoba, but it has that same look of a colonial, or rather provincial, city. We visited the consulate, where

---

*Spanish baroque architecture, characterized by elaborate surface decoration.

letters awaited us and, after reading them, went to see what we could do with an introduction we had for a bureaucrat at the Foreign Office, who, of course, didn't want to know us. We roamed from one police station to the next — until at one of them we got a plate of rice — and in the afternoon we visited Dr. Hugo Pesce, the expert leprologist, who welcomed us with extraordinary kindness for someone at the head of such a well-respected medical unit. He secured us lodging in the leprosy hospital and that night invited us to eat at his house. He turned out to be a fascinating conversationalist. It was very late when we got to bed.

It was also very late when we got up and had breakfast. There was apparently no "order" to feed us, so we decided to go down to Callao and visit the port. The going was very slow because it was May 1 and there was no public transport; we had to do the whole 14 kilometers on foot. There was nothing in particular to see in Callao, much less any Argentine boats. More bald-faced than ever, we presented ourselves at a police station and begged a bit of food, then beat a speedy retreat back to Lima. We again ate at Dr. Pesce's, who told us of his experiences with different types of leprosy.

In the morning we went to the Museum of Archaeology and Anthropology. Incredible, but a lack of time meant we couldn't see everything. The afternoon we dedicated to becoming familiar with the leprosy hospital,* with a guided tour by Dr. Molina, who, as well as being a good leprologist, is apparently an excellent thoracic surgeon. As was our custom by then, we went to eat at Dr. Pesce's.

We lost the whole of Saturday morning in the city center trying to change 50 Swedish crowns; we succeeded finally after a bit of hustling. We spent the afternoon exploring the laboratory, which didn't have much worth envying and, in fact, left a lot to be desired. The bibliographic records, however, were formidable in their clarity and method of organization and also in their comprehensive detail. At night, of course, we were off to Dr. Pesce's for dinner, and as al-

*The Hospital de Guia.

ways he proved his skill in animated conversation.

Sunday, an important day for us. Our first bullfight, and despite the fact that it went by the name of a *novillada*, a fight with lesser standard bulls and toreadors, we were hugely excited; so much so that I almost couldn't concentrate on one of Tello's books I was reading in the library that morning. We arrived as the bullfight was starting and just as we entered, a novitiate was killing the bull, but not in the normal way, by a *coup de grace*.* As a result the bull was suffering, laid out on the ground, while the toreador tried to finish it off and the public shouted. For the third bull there was considerable excitement when spectacularly it hooked the toreador and threw him to the air, but that was it. The fiesta closed with the almost unnoticed death of the sixth bull. Art, I see none; courage, a certain level; skill, not much; excitement, relative. In summary, it all depends what there is to do on a Sunday.

On Monday morning we again went to the museum. In the evening, to Dr. Pesce's house, where we met a professor of psychiatry, Dr. Valenza, another good talker who told us war anecdotes and others much like the following: "The other day I went to our local cinema to see a film with Cantinflas.** Everyone laughed but I understood nothing. But this was not unusual, as the rest of the people couldn't understand anything either. So, why were they laughing? In reality, they laugh at themselves, each one of them was laughing at a part of themselves. We're a young country, without tradition or culture, we've barely been discovered. And so they laugh at all of the blights that our infantile civilization has not been able to fix... But now then, has North America fully matured, despite its skyscrapers, its cars, its good fortune? Has it left its youth behind? No, the differences are in form only, they are not fundamental; all America is a sister in this. Watching Cantinflas, I understood Pan-Americanism!"

*In Spanish, *descabbeller:* to sever the bull's spinal cord with a dagger.
**Cantinflas was a prolific Mexican comic actor — a Mexican Charlie Chaplin.

Tuesday saw no change — in terms of museum visits — but at three in the afternoon we met with Dr. Pesce who gave Alberto a white suit and myself a jacket of the same color. Everyone concurs — we almost look human. The rest of the day was of no real importance.

Several days have passed and we have one foot in the stirrup, but remain uncertain as to when we will be leaving. We were supposed to leave two days ago, but the truck that is to take us hasn't left yet. The many parts that make up our journey are going well. In terms of furthering our knowledge, we visit museums and libraries. But the only one that really matters is the Archaeology and Anthropology Museum, founded by Dr. Tello. From a scientific perspective, leprosy that is, we have met Dr. Pesce; the others are merely his disciples and have a long way to go before producing anything worthwhile. Because there are no biochemists in Peru, the lab is run by specialist doctors and Alberto has spoken with some of them, putting them in touch with people in Buenos Aires. He got on well with two of them but the third person... Well, Alberto introduced himself as Dr. Granado, specialist in leprosy, etc., and they took him to be a medical doctor. So this silly guy he questioned, responded with: "No, there are no biochemists here. Just as there's a law prohibiting doctors from establishing pharmacies, we don't let pharmacists interfere in things they don't understand." Alberto was ready to get violent so I gently nudged him and this dissuaded him from doing so.

In spite of its simplicity, one of the things which left a very strong impression on us in Lima was the way the hospital patients farewelled us. They had all chipped in 100½ *soles*, which they gave to us along with an effusive letter. Afterwards some of them came to say goodbye to us personally and in more than one case tears were shed as they thanked us for the little bit of life we'd given them. We shook their hands, accepted their gifts, and sat with them listening to football on the radio. If there's anything that will make us seriously dedicate ourselves to leprosy, it will be the affection showed us by all the sick we've met along the way.

Lima as a city does not live up to its long tradition as a viceregal seat, but its residential suburbs are very pretty and spacious and so are its new streets. An interesting fact was the number of police surrounding the Colombian embassy. There were no less than 50 uniformed and plainclothes policemen doing permanent guard duty around the entire block.

The first day's journey out of Lima was unremarkable. We saw the road up to La Oroya and the rest we traveled during the night, arriving at Cerro de Pasco at dawn. We traveled in the company of the Becerra brothers, who, we called Cambalache* or Camba for short. They turned out to be very good people, especially the older one. We continued driving all day, descending into more pleasant places, and the headache and general feeling of ill-health I'd had since Ticlio, at 4,853 meters the highest point above sea level, started to improve. As we passed Huánuco and approached Tingo María, the front left axle broke, but luckily the wheel became stuck in the mudguard so we didn't turn over. That night we had to stay put. I needed to give myself an injection, but as luck would have it, the syringe broke.

The next day was uneventful and asthmatic, but that night fortune turned our way, when Alberto mentioned in a melancholic voice that today, May 20, was the six-month anniversary of our departure. That was the pretext for the *pisco* to flow. By the third bottle, Alberto stumbled to his feet, abandoned a little monkey he'd been holding in his arms, and disappeared from the scene. The younger Camba continued for another half a bottle, and crashed on the spot.

We left in a hurry the next morning, before the woman who owned the place woke up, because we hadn't paid the bill and the Camba brothers were short on cash because of repairs to the axle.

*Spanish for bric a brac, or junk store.

We drove the whole day until ending up stuck at one of those road barriers the army puts up to stop people traveling when its raining heavily.

The next day off again and we were detained once more at a barrier. Only in the evening did they let us move on, yet we were stopped again at a small town called Nescuilla, our final stop for the day.

The route was still closed the next day, so we went to the army post to get some food. We left in the afternoon, taking with us a wounded soldier, who would get us through the army roadblocks. Effectively, a few kilometers down the road, when the rest of the trucks were being stopped, ours was allowed through to Pucallpa where we arrived after nightfall. The younger Camba paid for our meal and to say goodbye we drank four bottles of wine that made him sentimental and he promised us his eternal love. He then paid for a hotel room for us to sleep in.

The main task at hand was getting to Iquitos; so we concentrated on that. The first person we hit on was the mayor, someone called Cohen; we had heard a lot about him, that he was Jewish as far as money was concerned but a good sort. There was no doubt he was tightfisted; the problem was whether he was a good sort. He palmed us off to the shipping agents, who in turn sent us to speak with the captain, who was kindly enough, promising the huge concession of charging us third-class fares and letting us travel in first. We weren't happy with this, and went to see the head of the garrison who said he couldn't do anything for us. Then the second-in-command, after interrogating us (and in doing so demonstrating his stupidity), promised to help.

We went for a swim that afternoon in the Río Ucayali which looks a lot like the Upper Paraná. We came across the deputy, who said he'd secured a great deal for us: as a special favor to him, the captain had agreed to charge us third-class fares and let us travel in first. Big deal.

There was a very rare pair of fish where we swam, called by the locals *bufeo*. Legend has it that they eat men, rape women and commit a thousand other acts of violence. Apparently it's a river dolphin, which among other strange characteristics, has genitals similar to those of a woman. So, the Indians use it as a substitute, but they must kill the animal once they've finished coitus because the genital area contracts and the penis cannot come out. That night we took on the ever arduous task of facing our colleagues at the hospital to ask for lodging. As expected, they greeted us coldly, and would have turned us away had our equanimity not won them over and we were given two beds where we could rest our weary bones.

UCAYALI ABAJO
down the ucayali

Carrying our packs, looking like explorers, we boarded the little boat *La Cenepa* just before it left. As agreed, the captain let us into first class where we quickly mingled with all the privileged passengers. After a few whistles, the boat pulled away from shore and so began the second stage in our journey to San Pablo. When we could no longer see the houses of Pucallpa and all that remained was a steady panorama of unbroken jungle, people began to leave the rails and gathered around the gambling tables. We approached with caution but Alberto was struck with momentary inspiration and won 90 *soles* at a card game called "21," very much like our "7½." This victory brought upon us the loathing of the other gamblers, because he had played with an initial stake of just one *sol* of the national currency.

On that first day we didn't have many opportunities for friendly exchanges with the other passengers and we kept somewhat to ourselves, not getting involved in the general conversation. The food was scarce and poor. The boat didn't sail at night because the river was too low. There were hardly any mosquitoes, and even though we were told this was normal we didn't really believe it, because by now we were used to the exaggerations (and understatements) people make when trying to deal with difficult situations.

Early the next morning, we were off. The day passed uneventfully, except for making friends with a girl who seemed rather easy; maybe she thought we had a few *pesos* despite the diligent tears we wept whenever there was any mention of money. Toward evening, when the boat docked by the riverbank, the mosquitoes came out in hordes to prove the tangible truth of their existence; attacking us in swarms throughout the night. Alberto covered his face with a piece of net and wrapped in his sleeping bag was able to get some sleep, but I began to feel the symptoms of an asthma attack, so between that and the mosquitoes, I didn't close my eyes until the morning. That night has escaped from my memory, but I do still remember feeling the skin on my butt that had taken on gigantic proportions from so many bites. I was sleepy the whole next day and stayed in some corner or other, trying to snatch a few winks in borrowed hammocks. My asthma showed no sign of abating and I had to take the drastic measure of getting asthma medicine by the banal method of paying for it. It relieved the attack slightly. We looked out dreamily beyond the river edge to the jungle, its inviting greenery so mysterious. My asthma and the mosquitoes restrained me somewhat, but virgin forests are so compelling for spirits like ours that physical impediments and all the nascent forces of nature only served to stimulate my desire.

The days passed with great monotony. The only form of entertainment was the game we couldn't enjoy fully because of our economic situation. Two more days went by uneventfully. This trip would normally take four days but the river was so low we had to stop every night; this delayed the journey and turned us into promising targets for the mosquitoes. Although the food is better in first class and the threat from mosquitoes less vicious, I'm not sure what we won in the bargain. We are drawn more to the simple sailors than to that small middle class which, whether rich or not, is too attached to the memory of what it once was to allow themselves the luxury of associating with two penniless travelers. They have the same crass ignorance as any other man, but the small victories they have achieved in life have gone to their heads, and their dull opinions are delivered with even more arrogance for the fact that they themselves have tendered them. My asthma worsened, though I was following my diet strictly.

A careless caress from that easy girl who showed sympathy for my pathetic physical state penetrated the dormant memories of my pre-adventurer life. That night as I was kept awake by the mosquitoes, I thought of Chichina, now a distant, intoxicating dream; though the dream's ending, unusual for this kind of naive reminiscing, leaves more honey than bitterness in my memory. I sent her a soft and unhurried kiss, that of an old friend who knows and understands her; then my mind took a road to Malagueño, that great hall of so many sleepless nights, where at that very moment she would probably be whispering her strange, composed phrases to some new suitor.

My eyes traced the immense vault of heaven; the starry sky twinkled happily above me, as if answering in the affirmative to the question rising deep within me: "Is all of this worth it?"

Two more days: nothing changed. The confluence of the Ucayali and the Marañon that gives birth to the earth's mightiest river has nothing transcendent about it: it is simply two masses of muddy water that unite to form one — a bit wider, maybe a bit deeper, but nothing else. I have no more adrenalin and my asthma is getting worse; I can eat only a handful of rice and drink *mate*. On the last day, close to arriving, we ran into a severe storm which meant we had to stop the boat. The mosquitoes swarmed around us in clouds, worse than ever, as if avenging us for the fact we would soon be out of their reach. It felt like a night without end, filled with frantic slaps and edgy yelps, endless card games like narcotics and with random phrases tossed out to maintain any conversation and to pass the time more quickly. In the morning, the fever of disembarking leaves one hammock lying empty and I lie down. As if enchanted, I feel as though a coiled spring is unwinding inside me, taking me to new heights, or into an abyss, I don't know which... Alberto wakes me with a rough shake. "Pelao,* we've arrived." The river had broadened to reveal in front of us a low lying town with some taller buildings, surrounded by jungle and reddened by the earth beneath them.

It was a Sunday, and our arrival day in Iquitos. We docked early at the pier and went directly to speak with the head of the International Cooperation Service. We did have an introduction to Dr. Chávez Pastor, but he was not in Iquitos. They were kind to us anyway, putting us up in the ward for yellow fever and giving us hospital food. My asthma was still bad and I couldn't get on top of my miserable wheezing, even with up to four injections of adrenalin a day.

The next day I felt no better and I spent it passed out in bed or rather "adrenalizing myself."

The following day I resolved to follow a strict morning diet and a more or less strict one at night, cutting out rice. I improved a little, though not much. At night, we watched "Stromboli" with Ingrid Bergman, and Rossellini as the director. You cannot give it any other rating besides bad.

Wednesday marked a distinctly important date for us with the

*Slang for "baldy."

announcement that we would be leaving the next day. The news made us significantly happier, since I had been unable to move because of my asthma and we spent days collapsed in bed.

Very early the next day we began to prepare psychologically to leave. The day passed, however, and we were still anchored; it was announced departure would be the following afternoon.

Confident that the owners' inertia could have us leaving later but never before time, we slept soundly and after taking a walk went to the library, where the assistant, extremely agitated, rushed in to tell us that *El Cisne* was sailing at 11:30 a.m. It was already 11:05. We gathered our things together quickly and, because I was still suffering from asthma, took a taxi which charged us half a Peruvian *libra* for Iquitos' eight blocks. We reached the boat and discovered it wasn't leaving until three, though it was required that we board by one. We weren't brave enough to disobey and go to eat at the hospital and, at any rate, it was more convenient not to, because now we could "forget" the syringe they had loaned us. We ate terrible and expensive food with an Indian belonging to the Yagua tribe, strangely attired in a red straw skirt and a few necklaces of the same straw; his name was Benjamín but he spoke almost no Spanish. Just above his left shoulder blade he had a scar from a bullet shot at almost point-blank range, because of "*vinganza,*"* according to him.

The night was brimming with mosquitoes fighting over our almost virgin flesh. There was an important addition to our psychological perspective in that trip when we learned it was possible to get from Manaos to Venezuela by river. The next day passed calmly, and we slept as much as possible to recover sleep lost to the hording mosquitoes. That night, at about 1 a.m., I was woken just seconds after I'd fallen asleep and told we had arrived in San Pablo. They advised the colony's medical director, Dr. Bresciani, who was very welcoming and facilitated a room for the night.

*A mix of Spanish and Portuguese for the word, "revenge."

QUERIDO PAPI
dear papi

Iquitos
June 4, 1952

The great riverbanks are full of settlements. To find savage tribes you must follow the tributaries deep into the interior — and, this time at least, we don't intend to make that journey. Infectious diseases have disappeared, but just in case, we've been vaccinated against typhoid and yellow fever and have good supplies of atebrine and quinine.

There are many diseases caused by metabolic disorders: the food available in the jungle is nutritionally inadequate, but you only become seriously ill by going without vitamins for over a week, and even if we went by river that's the longest period of time we would be without proper food. We're still not sure about this and have been looking into the possibility of flying to Bogotá, or at least to Leguisamo, from where the roads are good. It's not that we think it might be dangerous to travel by river, but to save money, which later on might be important for me.

Away from the scientific centers where we risk being exposed, our journey becomes something of an event for the staff of the leprosy hospitals and they shower us with the respect due to two visiting researchers. I've become really interested in leprology, but I don't know how long it will last. The patients in the Lima hospital farewelled us so wonderfully we were encouraged to carry on; they gave us a gas camping stove and managed to collect 100 *soles*, which for them in their economic situation counts as a fortune. Some of them had tears in their eyes when they said goodbye. Their appreciation sprang from the fact that we never wore overalls or gloves, that we shook their hands as we would shake anybody's, that we sat with them, talking about all sorts of things, that we played football with them. It may all seem like pointless bravado, but the psychological lift it gives to these poor people — treating them as normal human beings instead of animals, as they are used to — is incalculable and the risk to us extremely unlikely. Until today the only staff to have become infected are a medical orderly in Indochina who lived with his patients, and an overly zealous monk I would not like to vouch for.

LA COLONIA DE SAN PABLO
the san pablo leper colony

The following day, Sunday, we were up and ready to visit the colony, but to get there you have to go by river and, as it wasn't a working day, we couldn't go. So we visited the administrator of the colony, a butch looking nun called Mother Sor Alberto, then played a game of football in which the two of us performed very badly. My asthma began to recede.

Monday we sent a good proportion of our clothes to be washed, then went to the colony to visit the patients' compound. There are 600 sick people living independently in typical jungle huts, doing whatever they choose, looking after themselves, in an organization which has developed a rhythm and style of its own. There is a local official, a judge, a policeman, etc. The respect Dr. Bresciani commands is considerable and he clearly coordinates the whole colony, both protecting and sorting out disputes that arise between the different groups.

On Tuesday we visited the colony again, joining Dr. Bresciani as he made his rounds, examining the patients' nervous systems. He is preparing a detailed study of nervous forms of leprosy based on 400 cases. It really is very interesting work because many of the cases of leprosy in this region attack the nervous system. Actually, I didn't see a single patient who wasn't presenting such symptoms. Bresciani told us that Dr. Souza Lima was interested in early signs of nervous disorder among the children living in the colony.

We went to the part of the colony reserved for the healthy, where 70 or so people live. It is lacking basic amenities that are supposedly being installed, like electricity during the day, a refrigerator and even a laboratory. They are in need of a good microscope, a microtome, a technician — at the moment this post is occupied by Mother Margarita, nice but not very knowledgeable — and they need a surgeon to operate on nerves, eyes, etc. An interesting thing is that aside from the widespread nervous problems, there are very few blind people, perhaps leading to the conclusion that [indecipherable word] has something to do with it, seeing that most receive no treatment at all.

We repeated our rounds on Wednesday, passing the day with fishing and swimming in between. I play chess with Dr. Bresciani at night, or we chat. Dr. Alfaro, the dentist, is a wonderful person — relaxed and very friendly. Thursday is a day of rest for the colony so we changed our routine, not visiting the compound. We tried to fish, without success, in the morning. In the afternoon we played football and my performance in goal was less atrocious. On Friday I returned to the compound, but Alberto stayed to do bacilloscopes in the company of that sweet nun, Mother Margarita. I caught two species of *sumbi* fish, called *mota*, and gave one of them to Dr. Montoya to enjoy.

EL DÍA DE SAN GUEVARA
saint guevara's day

On Saturday, June 14, 1952, I, just a lad, turned 24, on the cusp of that transcendental quarter century, silver wedding of a life, which, all things considered, has not treated me so badly. Early in the morning I went to the river, to try my luck again with the fish, but that sport is like gambling: one starts out winning and ends up losing. In the afternoon we played football and I occupied my usual place in goal, with better results than on earlier occasions. In the evening, after passing by Dr. Bresciani's house for a delightful, huge meal, they threw a party for us in the dining room of the colony, with a lot of the Peruvian national drink, *pisco*. Alberto is quite experienced regarding its effects on the central nervous system. With everyone slightly drunk and in high spirits, the colony's director toasted us warmly, and I, "*piscoed*," replied with something elaborate, like the following:

> Well, it's my duty to respond to the toast offered by Dr. Bresciani with something more than a conventional gesture. In our presently precarious state as travelers, we only have recourse to words and I would now like to use them to express my thanks, and those of my traveling *compañero*, to all of the staff the colony who, almost without knowing us, have given us this beautiful demonstration of their affection, celebrating my birthday as if it were an intimate celebration for one of your own. But there is something more. Within a few days we will be leaving Peruvian territory, so these words have the secondary intention of being a farewell, and I would like to stress our gratitude to all the people of this country, who have unfailingly shown us their warmest hospitality since we entered Peru via Tacna.

I would also like to say something else, unrelated to the theme of this toast. Although our insignificance means we can't be spokespeople for such a noble cause, we believe, and after this journey more firmly than ever, that the division of [Latin] America into unstable and illusory nations is completely fictional. We constitute a single mestizo race, which from Mexico to the Magellan Straits bears notable ethnographical similarities. And so, in an attempt to rid myself of the weight of small-minded provincialism, I propose a toast to Peru and to a United Latin America.

My oratory offering was received with great applause. The party, consisting in these parts of drinking as much alcohol as possible, continued until three in the morning, when we finally called it a day.

Sunday in the morning we visited a tribe of Yaguas, the Indians of the red straw. After a 30-minute walk along a path, disproving all rumors about a dense, impenetrable jungle, we reached a group of huts where a family lived. Their way of living was fascinating — outside, beneath wooden planks and with tiny, hermetic palm frond huts to shelter in at night from the mosquitoes that attack in close formation. The women had abandoned traditional costume for ordinary clothes so you cannot admire their jugs. The kids have distended bellies and are rather scrawny but the older people show no signs of vitamin deficiency, in contrast with its rate among more developed people living in the jungle. Their basic diet consists of yucca, bananas and palm fruit, mixed with the animals they hunt with rifles. Their teeth are totally rotten. They speak their own dialect but some of them understand Spanish.

In the afternoon we played football and though I played better they got a sneaky goal past me. That night Alberto woke me with an acute stomach pain, which later was located in the right iliac cavity; I was too exhausted to preoccupy myself with someone else's strange aches so I advised he resign himself to the pain, turned over and slept till the next day.

Monday, the day medicine is distributed throughout the compound. Alberto, well-cared for by his dear Mother Margarita, was receiving penicillin religiously every four hours. Dr. Bresciani told me he was waiting for a raft to arrive with some animals, and that we could take some planks and make a small raft of our own. The idea inspired us and we started making plans to go to Manaos, etc. I had an infected foot, so I missed the afternoon game and instead chatted with Dr. Bresciani about everything imaginable and fell into bed very late.

Tuesday morning, with Alberto fully recovered, we went to the compound where Dr. Montoya had operated on the ulna in a leprous nervous system with apparently brilliant results, although the technique left much to be desired. We went to fish in the afternoon in a nearby lagoon, and caught nothing, of course; but on the way back I determined to swim across the Amazon. It took me nearly two hours to the great despair of Dr. Montoya who had no desire to wait so long. That night there was a jovial little party, ending in a serious fight with Señor Lezama Beltrán, an immature, introverted soul who was probably a pervert as well. The poor man was drunk and irate because he had not been invited to the party, so he started shouting insults and raving until someone punched him in the eye and gave him a beating as well. The episode upset us a little because the poor man, apart from being homosexual and a first-rate bore, had been very nice to us, giving us 10 *soles* each, bringing our total to: me 479, Alberto 163½.

Wednesday dawned to the rain, so we didn't go to the compound and the day was generally wasted. I read some García Lorca, and we went to see the raft tying up at the jetty. On Thursday morning, the day the medical staff have off, we went with Dr. Montoya to the opposite bank to buy food. We traveled down a branch of the Amazon, bought papayas, yucca, maize, fish, sugarcane at incredibly cheap prices, and fished a little. Montoya caught a regular fish and I got a *mota*. Coming back, a strong wind stirred up the river and the captain, Roger Alvarez, nearly wet his pants as the waves flooded his canoe. I asked for the rudder but he refused to give it to me and we went to the bank to wait for the river to calm down. Not until three in the afternoon did we get home. We cooked the fish but it didn't fully satisfy our hunger. Roger gave each of us a shirt and me a pair of pants, so my spiritual well-being improved.

The raft was almost ready, only needing oars. That night an assembly of the colony's patients gave us a farewell serenade, with lots of local songs sung by a blind man. The orchestra was made up of a flute player, a guitarist and an accordion player with almost no fingers, and a "healthy" contingent helping out with a saxophone, a guitar and some percussion. After that came the time for speeches, in which four patients spoke as well as they could, a little awkwardly. One of them froze, unable to go on, until out of desperation he shouted, "Three cheers for the doctors!" Afterwards, Alberto thanked them warmly for their welcome, saying that Peru's natural beauty could not compare with the emotional beauty of this moment, that he had been deeply touched, that he could say no more except... and here he extended his arms with Perón-like gesture and intonation, "I want to give my thanks to all of you."

The patients cast off and to the sound of a folk tune the human cargo drifted away from shore; the tenuous light of their lanterns giving the people a ghostly quality. We went to Dr. Bresciani's house for a few drinks, and after chatting for a while, to bed.

Friday was our day of departure, so in the morning we paid a farewell visit to the patients and, after taking a few photos, came back carrying two fine pineapples, a gift from Dr. Montoya. We bathed and ate, and close to three in the afternoon began to say our goodbyes. At half past three our raft, christened the *Mambo-Tango*, set off downstream carrying a crew of both of us, and also for a while Dr. Bresciani, Alfaro and Chávez who built the raft.

They took us out into the middle of the river and left us to fend for ourselves.

LA KONTIKITA SE REVELA
debut for the little kontiki

Two or three mosquitoes alone could not beat my desire to sleep and within a few minutes it had defeated them. My triumph was empty, however, in light of Alberto's voice shaking me from my delicious state of limbo. The faint lights of a little town, which from its appearance had to be Leticia, could be seen on the left bank of the river. What followed was the hugely arduous task of moving the raft toward the lights, and in this, we met with disaster: the contraption refused to go anywhere near the bank; intransigent, it was determined to set its own course down the middle of the river. We rowed at full strength and just when it seemed we were definitely on our way, we'd turn a half circle and head back into midstream. We watched with growing desperation as the lights drifted into the distance. Exhausted, we decided that at least we could win the fight against the mosquitoes and sleep peacefully until dawn, deciding what to do then. Our prospects were not very promising. If we continued down river we'd have to go as far as Manaos, a long way according to more or less reliable information, some 10 days' sailing. Due to an accident the day before, we didn't have any more fishing hooks, nor a great amount of essential provisions, and we weren't sure we could make it to the bank when we wanted to, without mentioning the fact that we'd entered Brazil without our papers in order and couldn't speak the language. But these concerns didn't worry us for too long, because very quickly we fell into a deep sleep. The rising sun woke me and I crawled out from under the mosquito net to determine our position. With the world's worst intentions, our little Kontiki had deposited itself on the right bank of the river, and was calmly waiting at a kind of little jetty belonging to a nearby house. I decided to put off inspecting things until later because the mosquitoes were still within eating range and were enjoying their feast. Alberto was sleeping deeply so I thought I'd join him and do the same. A morbid fatigue and an uneasy exhaustion overwhelmed me. I felt incapable of making any decision but clung to the thought that no matter how bad things became, there was no reason to suppose we couldn't handle it.

QUERIDA VIEJA
dear mama

Bogotá, Colombia
July 6, 1952

Dear Mama,

Here I am; my travels have taken me a few kilometers closer to Venezuela and made me a few *pesos* poorer. First, let me wish you the important happy birthday; I hope it was spent with love, laughter and the family. Next, I'll be organized and give you a concise account of my adventures since we left Iquitos. We set off more or less according to plan; traveling for two nights with our loyal retinue of mosquitoes and arriving in the San Pablo colony at dawn, where we obtained accommodation. The medical director, a marvellous guy, liked us immediately and we got on well with the whole colony generally, except the nuns who questioned why we never went to mass. These nuns ran the place and those who didn't attend mass had their rations reduced (we went without, but the kids there helped us and found us food every day). Apart from this minor cold war, life was incredibly pleasant. On the 14th, they gave me a party with lots of *pisco*, a kind of gin which makes you wonderfully drunk. The director of the colony toasted us and, inspired by the booze, I replied with a quintessentially Pan-American speech, winning great applause from the notable, and notably drunk, audience. We stayed a bit longer than planned, but finally left for Colombia. On the last night, a group of patients came over from the colony in a large canoe; they sang us farewell serenades on the jetty and made some very touching speeches. Alberto, who believes he is Perón's natural heir, delivered such an impressive, demagogic speech that our well-wishers were convulsed with laughter. It was one of the most interesting experiences of our trip. An accordion player who had no fingers on his right hand used little sticks tied to his wrist; the singer was blind; and almost all the others were horribly deformed, because of the nervous form of the disease very common in this area. With light from the lamps and the lanterns reflected in the river, it was like a scene from a horror movie. The place is lovely, surrounded completely by jungle, with indigenous tribes barely a mile away (whom we visited, of course), and a lot of fish and game to eat and incalculable potential wealth; all of this set us dreaming of crossing the Mato Grosso by river, from Paraguay to the Amazon, practising medicine along the way, and so on... a dream kind of like having your own home... perhaps one day... We were feeling more like authentic explorers and set sail downstream on a luxury raft they built especially for us. The first day went smoothly but that night, instead of keeping watch as we should have done, we both settled down to sleep, comfortably protected by a mosquito net we'd been given, and woke up the next morning to find we'd run aground on the riverbank.

We ate like sharks. That day passed cheerfully and we decided to alternate turns at keeping watch, by the hour, to avoid any more problems, since at dusk the current had carried us toward the bank and some half-submerged branches nearly caused the raft to capsize. I earned a demerit point during one of my watches, when one of the hens we were taking to eat fell into the river and the current swept it away. The man who had swum the full width of the river in San Pablo didn't have the courage to dive in after it, partly because we'd seen alligators surfacing every now and then, and partly because I've never really overcome my fear of water at night. If you'd been there you would have pulled it out and saved the chicken, so would Ana María, since you don't have ridiculous nighttime complexes like me.

One of our hooks caught the most enormous fish and we had a hard time hauling it on board. We kept watch till morning, when we moored at the bank and then crawled under the mosquito net, as there were particularly vicious mosquitoes about. After a good sleep, Alberto, who prefers fish to chicken, discovered our two baited hooks had vanished during the night, which put him in an even fouler mood. As there was a house nearby, we decided to find out how far it was to Leticia. When the owner told us in formal Portuguese that Leticia was seven hours upstream and that we were now in Brazil, Alberto and I had a furious argument over who had fallen asleep on watch. But this got us nowhere. We gave the owner the fish and a pineapple weighing about four kilos given to us by the lepers and stayed overnight in his house, before he took us upriver again. The return trip was quite fast, but hard work because we had to row for at least seven hours in a canoe and we weren't used to it. We found board and lodging, etc., at the police station in Leticia; but we couldn't get more than 50 percent off our airfares, and had to fork out 130 Colombian *pesos*, plus another 15 for excess baggage, making a total of 1,500 Argentine *pesos* in all. But what saved the day was that we were asked to coach a football team while waiting for the plane, which came only once a fortnight. At first, we only intended to coach them to the point where they wouldn't make fools of themselves; but they were so bad we decided to play, too. The amazing result was that what was considered the weakest team entered the one-day championship utterly reorganized, made it to the final and lost only on penalties. Alberto looked vaguely like Pedernera* with his spot-on passes, so he was nicknamed Pedernerita, in fact, and I saved a penalty which will go down in the history of Leticia. The whole celebration would have been great if they hadn't played the Colombian national anthem at the end and I hadn't bent down to wipe some blood off my knee during it, sparking a violent reaction from the colonel, who shouted at me. I was just on the edge of shouting back when I remembered our journey, etc., and bit my tongue. After a great flight in a cocktail-shaker of an airplane, we arrived in Bogotá. Alberto chatted to the other passengers on the way, recounting an awful flight we'd had across the Atlantic once when attending an international leprosy conference in Paris, and how three of the four engines had failed and we'd been within minutes of crashing into the Atlantic, concluding with, "Honestly, these Douglases..."; he was so convincing I was even scared myself.

We feel like we've been around the world twice. Our first day in Bogotá went pretty well, we found food on the university campus but no accommodation because it was full of students on grants for courses organized by the United Nations. No Argentines, of course. Just after one in the morning we finally found space at the hospital, by which I mean a chair to spend the night in. We're not terribly poor, but explorers with our history and stature would rather die than pay for the bourgeois comfort of a hostel. After that the leprosy service took us in, even though they had regarded us with suspicion the first day because of the letter of introduction we brought from Peru — very complimentary but signed by Dr. Pesce, who plays in the same position as Lusteau.** Alberto shoved various certificates under their noses and they hardly had time to catch their breath before I cornered them about my allergy work, leaving them reeling. The result? We were both offered jobs. I had no inten-

*Argentine footballer.
**Argentine footballer.

tion of accepting but Alberto, for obvious reasons, was considering it. I had been using Roberto's knife to sketch something on the ground in the street, and consequently we had an altercation with the police who harassed us so badly that instead of Alberto staying, both of us decided to leave for Venezuela as soon as possible. So by the time you get this letter, I'll be just about ready to leave. If you want to chance it, write to Cucuta, Santander del Norte, Colombia, or very quickly here to Bogotá. Tomorrow I'm off to see Millonarios play Real Madrid in the cheapest stand, since our compatriots are harder to tap than ministers. There is more repression of individual freedom here than in any country we've been to, the police patrol the streets carrying rifles and demand your papers every few minutes, which some of them read upside down. The atmosphere is tense and it seems a revolution may be brewing. The countryside is in open revolt and the army is powerless to suppress it. The conservatives battle among themselves and cannot agree, and the memory of April 9, 1948,* still weighs heavily on everyone's minds. In summary, it's suffocating here. If the Colombians want to put up with it, good luck to them, but we're getting out of here as soon as we can. Apparently Alberto has a good chance of finding work in Caracas.

I really hope someone will scribble a few lines to let me know how you are. You won't have to glean information through Beatríz or some other intermediary this time (I'm not replying to her because we're limiting ourselves to one letter per city, which is why the card for Alfredito Gabela is enclosed).

A huge hug from your son, who misses you from head to toe. I hope the old man manages to get himself to Venezuela, the cost of living is more than here, but the pay is much better and that should suit a skinflint (!) like him. By the way, if after living up here for a while he's still in love with Uncle Sam... but don't let's be diverted, Papi can read between the lines. Ciao.

---

*When the radical Liberal politician Jorge Eliecer Gaitán was murdered.

on the road to caracas

After the inevitable and unnecessary questions, the manhandling and fiddling around with our passports, and the inquisitorial stares, so suspicious as to be worthy of a police officer, the official stamped our passports with a big departure date of July 14, and we set out on foot across the bridge uniting and dividing the two countries. A Venezuelan soldier, with the same spiteful insolence as his Colombian counterparts — a common trait among all military stock, it seems — checked our luggage and then seized the opportunity to submit us to his own personal interrogation, just to show we were talking to someone with "authority." They detained us for a good while in San Antonio de Táchira but only for administrative formalities, and then we continued our journey in a van which promised to take us to the city of San Cristóbal. Halfway along the road is the customs post where we endured a thorough search of our entire luggage and our persons. The famous knife which had caused so much trouble in Bogotá returned, as the leit motif of a long discussion with the police chief. We conducted this discussion with an ease mastered through dealings with people of such high culture. The revolver was saved because it was inside the pocket of my leather jacket, in a bundle whose stench scared off the customs officers. The knife, recovered with such effort, was a new cause for concern because customs posts were placed all the way to Caracas and we weren't certain of being able to find brains capable of processing the elementary reasons we gave them. The road linking the two frontier townships is paved perfectly, especially on the Venezuelan side, and reminds me of the mountainous regions around Córdoba. In general, it seems that this country is more prosperous than Colombia.

On arriving in San Cristóbal, a fight broke out between the owners of the transport company and ourselves, who wanted to travel in the most economic way possible. For the first time in our trip, "their" thesis regarding the advantages of two days' traveling by van, rather than taking three days in a bus, won out. Eager to resolve our immediate futures and find proper treatment for my asthma, we decided to part with an extra 20 *bolívares*, sacrificing them in honor of Caracas. We occupied ourselves until evening, wandering around the neighborhood and reading a little about the country in quite a good library that's there.

At 11 p.m. we set off northward, leaving behind us all traces of asphalt. In a seat where three people were already squeezed in, they crammed in four of us, so there was no chance of sleeping. Even worse, a flat tire lost us an hour and my asthma was still bothering me. Wearily climbing toward the summit, the vegetation became scarcer, although in the valleys you could see the same types of crops growing as in Colombia. The roads were in a terrible state, causing many punctures; on our second day on the road we had several. The police have control points thoroughly checking all vans and we would have found ourselves in dire straits without the help of the letter of recommendation one woman passenger had — the driver claimed all the luggage was hers, mission accomplished. The price of a meal had risen and one *bolívar* per head became more like three and a half. We decided to save as much money as we could, so we fasted at the stop in Punta del Aguila, but the driver took pity on our indigence and gave us a good meal, at his expense. Punta del Aguila is the highest point of the Venezuelan Andes, reaching 4,108 meters above sea level. I took my two last remaining tablets with which I was able to get through the night. At dawn, the driver stopped for an hour to sleep. He had been driving for two days without a break. We expected to arrive in Caracas that night but flat tires delayed us again, as well as faulty wiring which meant the battery couldn't charge and we had to stop to fix it. The climate had become tropical and there were aggressive mosquitoes and bananas on all sides. The last stretch, during which I dozed, trying to cope with a decent asthma attack, was asphalted properly and seemed to be quite pretty (it was dark by then). As we arrived at our destination the sky was lightening. I was absolutely wrecked. I fell into a bed we rented for half a *bolívar* and slept like a tiger, aided by the substantial adrenalin injection given to me by Alberto.

ESTE EXTRAÑO SIGLO VEINTE
this strange twentieth century

The worst of my asthma attack has now passed and I feel almost well, though sometimes I resort to my new acquisition, a French inhaler. I feel Alberto's absence so sharply. It seems like my flanks are unguarded from some hypothetical attack. At every other moment I'm turning around to share an observation with him only to realize he's not there.

It's true, there's not really much to complain about: thoroughly looked after, good food and a lot of it, and the anticipation of returning home to start studying again and to obtain the degree which will enable me to practise. Yet the idea of splitting up definitively doesn't make me completely happy; the many months we've been side by side, through good and bad, accustomed to dreaming similar dreams in similar situations, have brought us so much closer together. With these ideas constantly turning over in my mind, I find myself drifting away from the center of Caracas. The homes in the suburbs are spaced much further apart. Caracas extends along the length of a narrow valley, enclosing and restraining it on its edges, so that on a short walk you'll be climbing the surrounding hills, and there, with the progressive city laid out before your feet, you'll begin to see a new aspect of its multifaceted makeup. The blacks, those magnificent examples of the African race who have maintained their racial purity thanks to their lack of an affinity with bathing, have seen their territory invaded by a new kind of slave: the Portuguese. And the two ancient races have now begun a hard life together, fraught with bickering and squabbles. Discrimination and poverty unite them in the daily fight for survival but their different ways of approaching life separate them completely: the black is indolent and a dreamer; spending his meager wage on frivolity or drink; the European has a tradition of work and saving, which has pursued him as far as this corner of America and drives him to advance himself, even independently of his own individual aspirations.

At this elevation the concrete houses have totally disappeared and only adobe huts reign. I peer into one of them. It is a room half separated by a partition, with a fireplace and table and a heap of straw on the ground, apparently serving as beds. Various bony cats and a mangy dog play with three completely naked black children. Rising from the fire, acrid smoke fills the room. The black mother, frizzy hair and sagging breasts, is cooking, assisted by a girl of about 15, who is dressed. At the door of the hut we get into a conversation and after a while I ask if they will pose for a photo, which they categorically refuse to do unless I give it to them straight away. In vain I try to explain that I have to develop it first, but no, they want it then and there, or no ball game. Eventually I promise to hand it over straight away, but now they are suspicious and don't want to cooperate. One of the kids escapes to play with his friends while I continue chatting with the family. In the end, I stand guard at the door, camera in hand, pretending to snap anyone who pokes out their head. We play around like this for a while until I see the little kid returning carefree on a new bicycle; I focus and press the button but the effect is disastrous. To elude the photo, the kid swerves and falls to the ground, bursting into tears. Immediately they all lose their fear of the camera and rush out to hurl abuse at me. I withdraw somewhat apprehensively because they are excellent stone throwers, followed by the insults of the group — including the height of contempt: "Portuguese."

Littered along the edges of the road are containers for transporting cars, used by the Portuguese as dwellings. In one of these, where a black family lives, I can just glimpse a brand new refrigerator, and from many of them radios blare music which their owners play at maximum volume. New cars are parked outside the most miserable "homes." All kinds of aircraft pass overhead, sowing the air with noise and silver reflections and there, at my feet, lies Caracas, city of the eternal spring. Its center is threatened by the invasion of red tiled roofs that converge with the flat roofs of modern buildings. But something else will allow the yellowy color of its colonial buildings to live on, even after they have disappeared from the city maps: the spirit of Caracas, impervious to the lifestyle of the North and stubbornly rooted in the retrograde semi-pastoral conditions of its colonial past.

The stars drew light across the night sky in that little mountain village, and the silence and the cold made the darkness vanish away. It was — I don't know how to explain it — as if everything solid melted away into the ether, eliminating all individuality and absorbing us, rigid, into the immense darkness. Not a single cloud to lend perspective to the space blocked any portion of the starry sky. Less than a few meters away the dim light of a lamp lost its power to fade the darkness.

The man's face was indistinct in the shadows; I could only see what seemed like the spark of his eyes and the gleam of his four front teeth.

I still can't say whether it was the atmosphere or the personality of that individual that prepared me for the revelation, but I know that many times and from many different people I had heard those same arguments and that they had never made an impression on me. Our interlocutor was, in fact, a very interesting character. From a country in Europe, he escaped the knife of dogmatism as a young man, he knew the taste of fear (one of the few experiences making you value life), and afterwards he had wandered from country to country, gathering thousands of adventures, until he and his bones finally ended up in this isolated region, patiently waiting for the moment of great reckoning to arrive.

After exchanging a few meaningless words and platitudes, each of us marking territory, the discussion began to falter and we were about to go our separate ways, when he let out his idiosyncratic, childlike laugh, highlighting the asymmetry of his four front incisors: "The future belongs to the people, and gradually, or in one strike, they will take power, here and in every country.

"The terrible thing is, the people need to be educated, and this they cannot do before taking power, only after. They can only learn at the cost of their own mistakes, which will be very serious and will cost many innocent lives. Or perhaps not, maybe those lives will not have been innocent because they will have committed the huge sin against nature; meaning, a lack of ability to adapt. All of them, those unable to adapt — you and I, for example — will die cursing the power they helped, through great sacrifice, to create. Revolution is impersonal; it will take their lives, even utilizing their memory as an example or as an instrument for domesticating the youth who follow them. My sin is greater because I, more astute and with greater experience, call it what you like, will die knowing that my sacrifice stems only from an inflexibility symbolizing our rotten civilization, which is crumbling. I also know — and this won't alter the course of history or your personal view of me — that you will die with a clenched fist and a tense jaw, the epitome of hatred and struggle, because you are not a symbol (some inanimate example) but a genuine member of the society to be destroyed; the spirit of the beehive speaks through your mouth and motivates your actions. You are as useful as I am, but you are not aware of how useful your contribution is to the society that sacrifices you."

I saw his teeth and the cheeky grin with which he foretold history, I felt his handshake and, like a distant murmur, his formal goodbye. The night, folding in at contact with his words, overtook me again, enveloping me within it. But despite his words, I now knew... I knew that when the great guiding spirit cleaves humanity into two antagonistic halves, I would be with the people. I know this, I see it printed in the night sky that I, eclectic dissembler of doctrine and psychoanalyst of dogma, howling like one possessed, will assault the barricades or the trenches, will take my bloodstained weapon and, consumed with fury, slaughter any enemy who falls into my hands. And I see, as if a great exhaustion smothers this fresh exaltation, I see myself, immolated in the genuine revolution, the great equalizer of individual will, proclaiming the ultimate *mea culpa*. I feel my nostrils dilate, savoring the acrid smell of gunpowder and blood, of the enemy's death; I steel my body, ready to do battle, and prepare myself to be a sacred space within which the bestial howl of the triumphant proletariat can resound with new energy and new hope.